Praise for *Creating the Urban Dream*

"With affordable housing among the most pressing challenges facing our nation, Charlotte developer Clay Grubb has written a compelling book that weaves his personal experiences together with common sense proposals to help more families live in safe homes while building wealth. Clay mixes a track record as an innovative, successful real estate investor with an obvious compassion to serve people with limited resources. The result is a book filled with credible suggestions that could produce marked progress in improving and expanding the American housing industry."

—David Mildenberg, editor, *Business North Carolina*

"Clay Grubb is a leader both in finding creative solutions to the affordable housing crisis and in challenging others to join the conversation. He balances his passion, deep knowledge, and experienced insight with the understanding that the voices and efforts of many are necessary to solve this problem. Most importantly, Clay Grubb is one of the most genuine, kind, authentic, and giving leaders I've ever met. His book provides straightforward, actionable tools for anyone who wants to improve their community and invest in a better future."

—Colonel Jimmy Blackmon, US Army (retired),
author of *Pale Horse* and *Cowboys over Iraq*

"Clay's book comes at the right moment—when we must, as a country, understand the social, political, and economic forces that brought us to the current crisis in affordable housing and create realistic options with local communities and developers to solve it."

—Ranji Nagaswami, investment industry leader, previously chief investment advisor, Bloomberg administration, City of New York

CREATING THE
URBAN
DREAM

Max,

   We will miss you.
Thank you for all you
did for Gmill Properties.

         Housing Matters!

CREATING THE
URBAN
DREAM

**TACKLING THE
AFFORDABLE HOUSING CRISIS
WITH COMPASSION**

Clay Grubb

ForbesBooks

Published by ForbesBooks, Charleston, South Carolina.
Member of Advantage Media Group.

ForbesBooks is a registered trademark, and the ForbesBooks colophon is a trademark of Forbes Media, LLC.

Printed in the United States of America.

10 9 8 7 6 5 4 3 2 1

ISBN: 978-1-94663-328-6
LCCN: 2019920982

Cover and layout design by George Stevens.

This publication is designed to provide accurate and authoritative information in regard to the subject matter covered. It is sold with the understanding that the publisher is not engaged in rendering legal, accounting, or other professional services. If legal advice or other expert assistance is required, the services of a competent professional person should be sought.

Advantage Media Group is proud to be a part of the Tree Neutral® program. Tree Neutral offsets the number of trees consumed in the production and printing of this book by taking proactive steps such as planting trees in direct proportion to the number of trees used to print books. To learn more about Tree Neutral, please visit **www.treeneutral.com**.

Since 1917, the Forbes mission has remained constant. Global Champions of Entrepreneurial Capitalism. ForbesBooks exists to further that aim by bringing the Stories, Passion, and Knowledge of top thought leaders to the forefront. ForbesBooks brings you The Best in Business. To be considered for publication, please visit **www.forbesbooks.com**.

This book is dedicated to the best team imaginable, the team that makes Grubb Properties an incredible place to be each and every workday. It is a team that never farms out the hard work, never strays from improving others' lives, and never gives up. Thank you for letting me play a role in your lives.

CONTENTS

ACKNOWLEDGMENTS

FOR DECADES I HAVE dreamed of writing a book, but housing was not the topic I imagined. Having finished this one, though, maybe the next one will be easier.

Only one person, Bea Wray, is truly responsible for this book's existence. She was hooked with the first story and immediately dubbed my style as "Andy Griffith meets Wall Street." She has pushed, coached, and occasionally ridiculed but has been an amazing inspiration. She introduced me to Bob Sheasley, who has patiently listened, edited, written and rewritten, edited and edited again. I am confident he is wondering why I didn't let him edit this section, but I owe a huge thank-you to Bob. He did a Herculean job helping me to get this across the finish line.

I would also like to thank my Aspen Institute Finance Leadership Fellows and their fearless leaders, Ranji Nagaswami, Jennifer Simpson, and Chris Varelas. They have committed to making this world a much better place through financial vehicles, and they have pushed me to make my impact. While this book was not the venture I committed to achieving, it certainly lays the groundwork. My venture goal is the creation of emergency lines of credit (ELC) for every homeowner with greater than an 80 percent mortgage. As Ranji says, "Life gets in the way sometimes." The goal of an ELC is to create a safety net for when life happens. As you will read, I have had a front-row seat for the rollercoaster ride that many families experience as they try to create a better life for their children, and I appreciate the need for compassion.

While I am indebted to many, it is the team at Grubb Properties that deserves the bulk of the credit. I have spent thirty years as a full-time team member and close to another decade as a part-time team member. They have been my family, my partners, and my inspiration for impacting the lives of so many who live and work in our properties. They have committed to protecting the hard-earned retirement accounts of thousands while refraining from the greed that grips so many in our industry. Compassion makes up the DNA of this team, and I could not be prouder to call myself a member.

I would also like to acknowledge the many people who have inspired me over the years:

My father, Bob Grubb, whom I was fortunate to have worked with most every afternoon from the time I was twelve until I went off to boarding school, along with many summers and vacations.

His sister, Lou Adkins, who poured energy into helping people advance their lives through homeownership. After working for Grubb Properties for decades, Lou joined Salisbury's Community Housing Coalition, helping countless families, and played a pivotal role helping many after the closing of the giant Pillowtex plant in Rowan County that laid off thousands in 2003.

My mother, Rochelle Grubb, who used to drive to Roanoke to hand out twenty-five dollars to every kid in our housing communities there who had a good report card. She inspired us to perfect our floor plans, making spaces elegant but efficient.

And I thank all the people who have volunteered their lives to these causes, like Bert Green, Delores Bailey, Mary Nell McPherson, and my childhood friend, Alex Hooker, who runs Boone's Habitat for Humanity.

Also, many elected officials are fighting for affordable housing, but one who stands out in my mind is Derwin Montgomery of Winston-Salem. He never backs down from pushing for more equity for those who need it most and at the same time asks me in every conversation whether there are things he can do to speed up permitting, building inspections, or other regulations to make housing construction more efficient and profitable. He demonstrates a rare balance of a desire for more regulation alongside the goal of leveraging capitalism.

Finally, none of this would occur without my ultimate critic who pushes me to second-guess every decision, my wife, Deidre. When I don't second-guess those decisions, she is happy to do it for me. Life with Deidre is never easy, never boring, and sometimes downright frustrating, but there isn't a human being with a bigger heart. Her generosity for those in her life knows no limits, and it is truly amazing. I like to think I am naturally well-intentioned, but I have to stop and process everything. Deidre's generosity and love are never reasoned; they are just given blindly. As a result, Deidre did amazing work leading Charlotte's Habitat for Humanity family services and family selection committees for many years while also serving on that board for close to a decade. Imagine how wonderful this world would be if we could all find that childlike instinct to share. She has been a true inspiration for me.

Of course, my son, Davis, and my daughter, Rosalie, are my greatest source of inspiration. I am so proud of them, and I hope that my commitment to finish this book will inspire them to push to improve the world beyond my capabilities and dreams.

Thank you for reading my story! I hope it inspires you to improve your community and find ways to house and create economic mobility opportunities for everyone.

—Clay

ON THE BRINK
OF A CRISIS

> *The free market is ruled, not by the consumers,*
> *but by the producers. The most successful ones*
> *are those who discover new fields of production.*
>
> **Ayn Rand**

TO QUOTE AYN RAND seems an unlikely start to a book focused on affordable housing in today's market, but I think it is more than appropriate. The issue with the lack of economic mobility and housing equity in America stems from centuries of abuse by the white bourgeoisie. Richard Rothstein's recent book, *The Color of Law: A Forgotten History of How Our Government Segregated America,* is an eye-opening read into how our federal government not only encouraged segregation but, in many cases, mandated it. As a result, it is estimated that 98 percent of home loans in America went to white families from 1934 to 1968, a time when home equity was the primary, if not the only, source for most families to create wealth to pass to the next generation.[1] The black American was precluded whenever possible from achieving the Horatio Alger dream.

We now find ourselves in a period with tremendous demand for new housing but with inadequate production, something that just feels downright un-American. Why is that happening, and how did we get here? In this book, I share my experiences and some potential solutions.

I started working in the housing industry at age twelve, collecting mortgages from predominantly African American families that would otherwise not have had an opportunity to own a home and create equity for their children. The company my father founded had a positive impact on hundreds of families. Unfortunately, charlatans and swindlers convinced many other hardworking families to purchase homes they could not afford, with usurious rates and penalties. For them, success became unattainable.

Today's housing problem is estimated to eclipse $1 trillion, yet our government keeps trying to tackle the problem with the same agencies and policies that were created during the Jim Crow era and resulted in today's problem. Our government, while the best on the planet, is far from efficient when it comes to solving many problems—but capitalism made America great, and we must rely on it to solve our greatest problems.

That doesn't mean government shouldn't have a role, as most Republicans proclaim. The impacts of over a century of discrimination are real. Every child needs a safe and secure home to grow and become a productive member of society. Government must create incentives and regulations to enhance living opportunities, integration, and economic mobility. However, unlike what most Democrats

1   Richard Rothstein, *The Color of Law: A Forgotten History of How Our Government Segregated America* (New York: Liveright, 2017).

2

argue, government ownership, production, and other direct roles in housing often hinder those goals and almost always use capital inefficiently. I write these statements not to upset Republicans and Democrats but to encourage bipartisan efforts to address the crisis. It is the best of both ideologies that will allow us to prevail, not myopic policies of the past.

> **It is the best of both ideologies that will allow us to prevail, not myopic policies of the past.**

Since I began writing this book, the government has created eight thousand seven hundred opportunity zones across the nation in an experiment to leverage the best of capitalism with a focus on the most challenged neighborhoods. There will be winners and there will be losers, but the one guarantee of this new legislation is that there will be change. Gentrification will push many people from their homes and neighborhoods, but on the other hand it will create instant wealth for those families lucky enough to own their homes in these census tracts.

One of those opportunity zones is the Historic West End neighborhood in Charlotte, where 27 percent of the families own their homes. One of our African American elected officials owns the historic Excelsior Club, a black nightclub that hosted Nat King Cole and Louis Armstrong. According to the *Charlotte Observer*, it could have been purchased in 2018 by the County for $350,000, but the price was rejected as too expensive. Today, that same club is expected to sell for over $1.2 million, almost exclusively because it is in an opportunity zone. That example is not unique among opportunity zone locations. One of the residents of the Historic West End shared the story of a neighbor's house selling for $16,000 and shortly thereafter reselling for more than $200,000, with the newest owner now asking over $300,000 for that same home. Opportunity zone legislation has got the capitalist juices flowing for many, with a goal of creating significant wealth in neighborhoods that have long been neglected.

Of course, the problem is that 73 percent of the families in the Historic West End rent their homes, as is the case in many other opportunity zones. They don't have any equity or ownership stake to allow them to participate in the value creation. What will they do, where will they live? Their homes are likely to be purchased by speculators hoping to improve the property and flip it for a profit or rent it for significant premium to its current rate. That is the terrible side of gentrification, and it is one that will be devastating for thousands of families as they are forced economically from their homes and neighborhoods.

In the Historic West End, Grubb Properties has designated 10 percent of its 2019 Qualified Opportunity Fund dollars to help those facing the pains of gentrification. We will try to come up with novel ways to aid families that want to stay in the neighborhood but cannot afford the rapid escalation in rent that comes with modern development. The Knight Foundation, the Local Initiatives Support Corporation, Self-Help Credit Union, the Federal Reserve, and many others are engaging in the conversation to come up with ways to minimize the negative impacts that come from thousands of families being uprooted from the neighborhoods they have called home for generations.

There is no silver bullet to solve today's housing affordability crisis.

There is no silver bullet to solve today's housing affordability crisis. It is a fundamental imbalance of having more demand for homes than we have supply, a deficit estimated at close to four million homes. This shortage is causing home prices and rents for working families to skyrocket. At Urban Institute's recent housing affordability brainstorming session, it was quoted that the number of families in the United States paying over 50 percent of their income in rent was believed to exceed nineteen million.

As Ayn Rand states, "The action to sustain human life is primarily intellectual: everything man needs has to be discovered by his mind and produced by his effort." Government's role needs to be in promoting environments for the private sector to produce homes, manage them, and encourage equity opportunities for those interested and willing to participate.

We must face this problem with a balance of compassion and competence. The solution will require plenty of both, and the efforts of many. Economic mobility benefits all of us and makes America stronger, healthier, and safer.

CHAPTER 1

A FOUNDATION OF COMPASSION

> We are in this world to delight others.
>
> **Adam Robinson**

"ELLISON MCINTOSH WILL BE here to see you soon," Mary Haggerty, my assistant, said as she stepped into my office. "You need to be here."

I paused to reflect on that name, which I hadn't heard in years. "Ellison McIntosh? He's coming down from Lexington? Can't you handle it?"

"No, you need to handle this one. He will be here in about an hour," she said as she left my office with a sly smile on her face.

It felt odd. As the chief executive officer of Grubb Properties, I was extremely busy, and Mary always took pride in dealing with issues on my behalf. How could one mortgagee, whose house payment was probably less than $600 a month, warrant taking time from my busy day? Why didn't he just call me?

I had lived in Charlotte for over a dozen years, ever since I returned to the real estate company after graduating from law school. I had helped expand our operations from Lexington, my hometown, to the much larger city of Charlotte. Our new offices in Charlotte were on the edge of downtown in a new building we had recently developed as part of a larger vision to revitalize the Elizabeth Avenue corridor. In fact, Barack Obama's campaign offices were downstairs, and I got to meet him there on the eve of his initial presidential victory.

By 2007, Grubb Properties wasn't much into the mortgage business anymore. That had been our foundation when my father launched the company more than four decades earlier by building single-family houses and providing financing for families that had been excluded from the all-white world of bank loans. Since then, we had turned our focus to commercial properties as well as multifamily housing, with increasing emphasis on urban rental communities.

But we still handled a few mortgages that originated in the company's early years. As a boy, I helped my dad and learned the business by collecting mortgages on some of those early homes in Lexington. Recalling that time helped me better place where I first met Ellison McIntosh. He was one of those homeowners. I recalled back in those days, we had seen his family through some challenging times.

But that was, what, a quarter century ago, I thought. *Why's he coming all this way, driving sixty miles and fighting the Charlotte traffic, to see me? How does he even remember me? I wonder what could be so important? I hope this isn't bad news.*

"They are here to see you now," Mary said. It had seemed that only minutes had gone by as I daydreamed about the past. "I put them in the executive conference room."

They? I wondered what she meant. Stepping into the conference room, I found Ellison there with two of his children and three of his grandchildren. "Mr. Grubb?" he said, as he looked at me nervously. "I wanted to hand deliver you my final mortgage payment." Then he gave me a check.

I was at a loss for words. It had been thirty years to the month since he had started making payments on the mortgage for one of the houses that my father built in his redlined neighborhood. Ellison was here to make his 360th and final installment. He would now own his home outright, and he wanted his kids and grandkids to see for themselves how important this occasion was. He wanted them to know that things work out if you do what's right and keep a steady eye on the future. This was no small accomplishment. Here was a family that had achieved nothing less than the American Dream that so many deserving families had been denied.

His grandkids sat quietly around the table. They were young, about my age when I had been working with their granddaddy back in Lexington. I could see Ellison's pride as he handed me the check. He was an amazing example for his family. He had given his loved ones a legacy of security and equity.

I felt proud of the role that my father had played in helping hundreds of families beat the odds stacked against them. Dad did what few others would venture to do, which was to go against the grain making home loans to folks shut out of the system. Ellison McIntosh's success represented my father's legacy too.

"Thank you," I stuttered. I wish I had thought to say something more, but I had not a clue what to do. I wasn't even prepared to have his mortgage there to mark it canceled, much less do something more ceremonial. I was astounded that his family had come with him to deliver the final payment—and I will treasure the memory of that moment forever.

THE SHIFTING AMERICAN DREAM

The research verifies what common sense tells us: Those who grow up feeling safe and secure in a home with support are much more likely to become productive members of society. A sense of insecurity in childhood, whether emotional or physical, can severely hamper the ability to learn, grow, and operate in the world.

Those who grow up feeling safe and secure in a home with support are much more likely to become productive members of society.

Although we celebrate stories of people who have thrived despite a fractured home life in a rough neighborhood, those rags-to-riches tales are by far the exception. A lot is at stake. Substandard housing hurts our families and children. An ample supply of decent, affordable homes is critical to a healthy and prosperous society.

For generations, homeownership has been an avenue toward a better life. By building equity in a place that they could call their own, families advanced and grew in wealth. As the value of the home increased, so did the pride of ownership—and that value and pride were both assets to strengthen the next generation. Many families prospered from that opportunity. Many families did not. They were left out and kept down, often purposefully, by a society inclined to push them to the margins.

My father showed a personal touch that the lending industry lost over the years. He understood what he called "the bumps in the road," such as a factory worker's broken leg that prevented him from earning his paycheck and making his monthly mortgage payments. If you don't hit one of those bumps now and then, you must not be alive and moving. We all need a little help sometimes along the way, and the computerized, syndicated, and overregulated world of today fails to appreciate that fact.

A lot of lenders once exercised discretion to show compassion, whether they were extending loans to home buyers or small businesses. When Ben & Jerry's opened their first ice cream shop in Vermont, they had a booming summer, but in the grip of winter it was hard to make the loan payments. Their bank understood and waived their principle payments until they hit their stride again the next summer—and an institution was born.

The human touch faded as the lending industry began to package, sell, and resell home loans, syndicating them far and wide through mortgage-backed security programs. When homeowners hit a bump, who would sit down to chat with them? They couldn't find anybody with the authority to negotiate the loan. Their only choice was to make that payment or face foreclosure. Yes, the industry should enforce responsibility and discipline, but it need not be heartless.

That loss of humanity led to the well-documented abuse of the system that caused the housing meltdown and contributed to the global financial crisis in 2008. Millions lost their homes. In the aftermath, the industry swung to the other extreme, overregulation. The result of the federal government's crackdown on home loans was that even hardworking people with decent credit couldn't qualify for mortgages at the best time in history to buy a home, when they were cheapest. That effectively kept millions of lower- and middle-class families from enjoying the equity that a home could have built.

AN EMERGENCY LINE OF CREDIT

One of my main initiatives, which I have been working on with the Aspen Institute, where I am a finance leadership fellow, is to create a mandatory home equity line of credit for all home loans with greater than 80 percent financing. The idea is simple: set up a 5 percent emergency line at the initial financing of the home purchase.

The line of credit would be maintained by the loan origi-nator, making sure it had skin in the game and wouldn't just approve any home loan. The amortization schedule would be shorter term, like five years, so that it would be available for the next emergency. In addition, there would be specific guidelines on when the line could be used—such as medical emergencies, natural disasters, or something as simple as a tree falling on one's house.

The emergency line of credit would be good not only for the homeowner but also for the investor, providing a backstop against a lapse in payment when life happens. It would be a security net providing peace of mind for hardworking families. The investor would gain a sense of security, which often results in lower pricing that helps to make housing more affordable. The investor also would feel reassured that the loan originator did due diligence. To entice originators to offer this option, I would propose that Fannie and Freddy waive the clawback on the loans they purchase that come with this provision.

Another benefit is that these second mortgages would help to ward off predatory lenders. It's naive to think that regulations alone can stop them. However, putting them third in line to collect on a debt and even banning their ability to foreclose would certainly reduce the problem.

In Charlotte, I helped Habitat for Humanity come up with their soft second mortgage program, which successfully reduced the number of instances folks fell prey to predatory lenders. The idea was that Habitat, which would sell the homes at cost without interest on the mortgages, would add an additional $10,000 second mortgage that would go away after 15 years of payments on the first mortgage. However, they would get paid the additional $10,000 prior to a third lien holder, should one exist and try to foreclose, or if the house sold prematurely for a profit. This protected Habitat as well as the homeowner.

The primary objection I hear to the creation of ELCs is the risk of additional leverage when one is facing financial challenges; however, the reality is when crisis hits, that is when money is most precious. JP-Morgan Chase just released a lot of their statistics from the 2008 global financial crisis, and the one that stood out the most for me was the fact that defaults were not tied to the amount of equity in a home or even the amount of leverage; they were tied to ability to pay. People that were underwater were willing to pay if they could, and those with substantial equity were unwilling to pay if they could not afford the monthly costs. To me, this is the strongest evidence of why we should continue to promote homeownership for those less fortunate and provide them safety nets to get through the moments when life happens.

Meanwhile, house prices have gotten out of reach for many. The real estate website Trulia reports that in Raleigh, North Carolina, a first responder earning the median salary for that profession in 2019 could afford just 11.1 percent of homes for sale in that market. In 2014, he or she could have afforded 30 percent of the available homes.[2] The trend of rising home prices is only accelerating, putting housing beyond the reach of significant sectors of the workforce, just as the millennials are starting their careers and seeking out homes.

When people no longer dream of buying a home, or never buy into the dream to begin with, what do they do instead? They rent a home. Today, those renters include a mix of the working class who are struggling to gain better footing, the up-and-coming millennials who want freedom of movement, and the retiring baby boomers who are ready to downsize. The ranks of renters also include many of those who were stung in the housing meltdown and either have failed to recover or who have lost their desire for homeownership.

A lot of folks from many walks of life, in other words, are looking for an apartment these days—and they want apartments in urban areas near job opportunities, entertainment, and other amenities. And many are going to keep on looking. As demand pushes up prices, the cost of living has risen significantly. They are finding it a lot harder to get a place that they can afford.

The shortage of affordable housing in our urban areas will have the consequence of further stifling social and economic mobility. Many who live in the poorer urban neighborhoods are finding that they are getting pushed out by gentrification. Those who need to be in the city to advance their careers are finding that they simply cannot afford to live there—or, if they do manage to pay the high rent, they are unable to save for anything else.

Once, a high school kid could get a good job in a factory and

---

2   Cheryl Young, "Making a Housing Wage: Where Teachers, First Responders and Restaurant Workers Can Live Where They Work," Trulia Research, May 2, 2019, https://www.trulia.com/research/housing-costs-teachers/.

stay there until retiring. In today's global economy, that factory is likely to morph into something else soon or leave town entirely. No job there seems secure for long. The ones who are coping quite well in this high-velocity environment are those who have embraced higher education. Their families are enjoying a net worth that is greater than ever in history.

Many of the successful ones have found their niche in this new age of information and technology. They tend to want to reside in urban environments where they are most likely to find the facilities to further their education and to make the connections that will advance their careers.

Social media and job networking sites have broadened the scope of employment opportunities. Not all that long ago, a job hunter in Kalamazoo would browse the help-wanted ads in the newspaper for a position with a local employer. Today, he or she can browse the internet and quickly find openings in Spokane, Tampa, or Cincinnati.

The option of renting is important to people who want to readily go wherever their careers might take them for a better job or a promotion. In other words, folks who are interested in advancing their careers want to be able to move—that is, if they can afford it.

In the metamorphosis of the American Dream, millions of people have turned from buying a place of their own to renting a place of their own. As the shortage of affordable apartments reaches crisis proportions, those folks could be in for a big disappointment. Decent, secure housing, so essential to a healthy society, may be far beyond their reach, if they can find it at all.

CREATING VIBRANT, DIVERSE COMMUNITIES

To get to know your neighbors is to live a richer life. We miss out on so much when we fail to interact with people who look or talk or worship differently. When instead we count them among our friends, understanding and compassion have a chance to grow. We have less tolerance for intolerance.

The urban environments of America tend to offer a diversity of race, ethnicity, and religion among people of differing social and economic standing. In our cities live the wealthy, the poor, and the multitude in the middle. Within urban borders is a cross section of the world's people.

In most of America, they do not generally live in the same neighborhoods. Nationwide, the housing stock has long been largely segregated. The well-to-do have their gated communities where not just anyone can gain access. Others may have been relegated, in one way or another, to the grayer, dirtier parts of town that have been variously called ghettos, slums, barrios, hoods, or projects. For generations, the neighborhood boundaries have been drawn along racial, ethnic, and economic lines. It's white people over here, black people over there. Folks with money here; folks without, stay out.

Our society suffers from the compulsion to put up those fences.

Our society suffers from the compulsion to put up those fences. Segregation limits access to opportunity. Whatever keeps people apart will also keep some of those people down. The concept of "separate but equal" inevitably makes some more equal than others. The resources that refine us should be within reach of us all.

To that end, the policies of our institutions, and of government at all levels, must promote inclusion. That was not, however, the longstanding policy of our federal government or even our state and local governments. We tend to put lower-income people of similar economic and social standing into public housing projects where economic and social mobility is virtually nonexistent.

One of the more recent mistakes in public housing policy has been the siphoning off of the older population. Senior housing has been the craze for the past two decades, as we have escorted grandparents to segregated accommodations. This has eliminated what is called "the grandmother effect" from many public housing communities. When a lot of kids are roaming the streets without the oversight of responsible elders, trouble is pretty much inevitable.

Grubb Properties has a lower-income property in Richmond, Virginia, where we have retained a significant number of grandparents by capping how much rents can increase for families that have lived on the property for five years or more, a policy implemented at all our multifamily communities. We voluntarily implemented the program to make sure we had a stable and diverse neighborhood. There, with the grandmothers keeping an eye on things, a couple of teenagers firing up a joint in the parking lot wouldn't have a chance. Within thirty seconds, one grandmother would be hollering out the window at them. Within a minute, another would be calling the police, and ninety seconds later a third might be dragging each of those kids by the ear across the parking lot and delivering a strict lecture.

With the elders around, the environment is safer, and lessons on behavior and other important factors get passed down to the next generation. In such an environment, people take pride in improving their lives. Most of our government policies, however, tuck older folks away by themselves in a high-rise somewhere. They lose the benefit of youthful energy in their daily lives—and they aren't around to make sure the young people behave.

Communities thrive when they have a healthy mix of people of differing backgrounds, ages, and cultures, as cities worldwide are experiencing. We learn from one another. Compassion and empathy grow when people of means live next to people who sometimes struggle to pay their bills. Our differences should enrich us, not separate us. One new friendship at a time, we can help to pull down barriers that divide neighborhoods and nations.

That is why Grubb Properties has turned away from building purely luxury communities or exclusively affordable housing neighborhoods. We strive to include spaces for the working class with modest incomes alongside the many wealthy people that are still attracted by our thoughtful developments. We believe keeping apartment rents reasonable is the best way to encourage economic diversity.

We often kept diversity in mind while planning earlier developments, but we didn't loudly promote it out of concern that it would hurt the image of a project. In 2003, we built The Ratcliffe, Charlotte's first condominium high-rise with $1 million-plus condominiums. We included fourteen units that we sold for less than $200,000, something few folks knew about, including many who purchased condominiums in the building. That project attracted some of the most visible buyers in the market at the time: Bob Johnson, who had just bought Charlotte's NBA franchise after making a fortune creating Black Entertainment Television; Rodney Peete, the Charlotte Panthers quarterback, along with his wife, actress Holly Robinson, who was on the cover of TV Guide the month they bought the condominium; and arguably North Carolina's most famous active athlete at the time, NASCAR driver Jeff Gordon.

Our aim is to create vibrant communities of interesting people with a variety of pursuits in life. By getting to know one another, they can discover opportunities to advance that otherwise might never have come their way. More and more people today desire to live in diverse communities rather than in neighborhoods where everybody seems the same as everyone else. Fortunately, the millennial generation appears to be resisting historical segregation patterns adopted by earlier generations, and neighborhood diversity is on the rise in America.

STANDING TOGETHER

In the years before the crash of the housing market and the economic crisis of 2008–09, the concept of character seemed to be disappearing from mortgage underwriting. It became a digital, computer-generated process that people learned to manipulate for profit. The excesses in the industry led to millions of people losing their homes.

The reaction to abuse tends to be an increase in regulation, which can be just as harmful as underregulation. Reasonable regulations can help the housing industry promote fairness and opportunity. The dream has slipped away from so many people, time and time again, and the government must be vigilant and take action when necessary. For example, the Fair Housing Act of 1968 and its update in 1988 prohibited discrimination based on race, color, religion, sex, disability, family status, and national origin. These are steps in the right direction, but we must continue to promote and preserve essential protections.

However, we should not overregulate to the point where even a hardworking person with a stable job can't get a home loan, as happened in the wake of the housing crash. The rules can go too far. The government clamps down, then eases up for fear of stifling prosperity. The pendulum swings, and it usually overswings. In one direction, you can get a mortgage if you're alive and breathing. In the other, you might try—but don't hold your breath. What we need is sensible balance and a renewed emphasis on character, for both borrower and lender. We must promote opportunity. Compassion should always play a role.

I think again of Ellison McIntosh and what he represented. He brought his loved ones along so that they could watch him pay off his mortgage and fulfill a family legacy. After years of diligence, he realized his dream. Were it not for my father's intervention, however, he might never have had the opportunity to take the first step.

My father put a premium on compassion, and at Grubb Properties we have worked hard to maintain that approach. It's what our nation and our communities need as we strive to resolve the housing crisis that we now face. It's high time that we invest in the future. Together we must provide good homes for the many people who need them, and we must put those homes in dynamic neighborhoods where they can better their lives. That is our huge challenge for many years to come—and a huge opportunity for those who will join in helping to solve it.

CHAPTER 2

SNAPSHOT OF AFFORDABLE HOUSING

> Our vision: a world where everyone has a decent place to live.
>
> **Habitat for Humanity**

CHERLONDA WAS NINE YEARS old when we met her, a charming little girl who lived across the street from the first Habitat house that my wife and I helped to build in Charlotte. Today, Cherlonda is in her late twenties, an enterprising young woman whose story illustrates so much about the power of community and compassion.

It was just before the turn of the millennium when Cherlonda's mom, Andromeda, moved her family into one of a hundred homes that Habitat for Humanity built in Charlotte's Belmont neighborhood. Habitat was trying to stabilize the crime-ridden neighborhood by bringing homeownership to it, as they do with communities around the world. My wife, Deidre, became Cherlonda's mentor as part of a newly launched mentorship program. Deidre and Cherlonda, along with Cherlonda's sister Unique and her mentor Trish, would end up gracing the cover of the Habitat International millennial calendar the following year.

Photo from the cover of the Habitat International millennial calendar.

We welcomed Cherlonda, Unique, their brother B.J., and Andromeda to spend time with our family. That relationship paid dividends both ways. One of the most impactful moments was during our daughter Rosalie's first morning of kindergarten. We had decided to send her to a public school miles away. She was the only kid from our upper-income neighborhood to attend the school despite its national reputation for language immersion. Of course, I wanted her to ride the bus too. I strongly believe in the importance of social education and I felt the bus ride was an important part of a well-rounded education.

"It's her first day there, though," Deidre protested. "We should drive her there just for today." But I insisted that she should start off the same way as most children. "OK, so you're in charge this morning," Deidre said, reaching for her keys to drive our son Davis to school. She paused to write "847" on a large card and attach it to Rosalie's backpack. "This is her bus number. Don't let her get on any bus but that one. I mean it. I want you to promise that you won't put her on any bus but 847, no matter what happens." I promised.

An hour after the scheduled arrival time, bus 673 pulled up and screeched to a halt. "Is she going to Smith Academy?" the bus driver growled as the door snapped open. I hesitantly nodded my head yes. "Put her on, I'm running late," the driver barked.

"But … but this isn't the right bus number," I mumbled.

"Get her on here right now," she insisted. "That bus broke down and I'm an hour late and don't have time for games." I stammered, the driver glared, I obliged. Rosalie hopped up the steps, and the door slammed shut. As the bus lurched forward and disappeared down the street, I felt as if Freddie Krueger from *Nightmare on Elm Street* had just departed with my precious five-year-old daughter and I would never see her again.

When I got home, I told Deidre the bus had been late. She said, "It was bus 847, right?" I tried to explain how that bus had broken down, but she panicked. "How could you be so irresponsible? You promised!" She called the school and, after much drama, the school was able to confirm that bus 847 had broken down and there had been a replacement bus. However, anxiety ran high for the remainder of that day as we were not able to confirm Rosalie's safe passage to her class.

At four o'clock, bus 673 pulled up at the bus stop a block from our house and Rosalie hopped out with a big smile on her face. Deidre was so relieved to see our daughter safe again. She hugged her and said, "Are you OK?" Rosalie looked at her and said, "Of course." Deidre asked how her first day of school had gone. Rosalie said, "Mom, it was great. Shanique was on the bus." (Rosalie was too young to pronounce Unique's real name.) "I sat with her, and she walked me to my class. School was so much fun."

As tears rolled down Deidre's face, she could not have been more thankful for the relationship we had with Cherlonda's family. We were embarrassed that we had never thought about Unique being on the same bus. But we were both thrilled to know that Unique, who was ten at the time, would be on the bus every day with Rosalie and that Rosalie would have a friend we trusted to look after her.

As big sister Cherlonda grew into adolescence, her goal in life was to have children. She had her first at age fifteen and her second at seventeen, then she dropped out of high school. Deidre kept questioning what more she might have done as Cherlonda's mentor, but she stayed faithful to the relationship. She is a natural nurturer, more patient than me.

For a time, in fact, I was livid. After Cherlonda's first pregnancy and miscarriage, I had offered her mother Andromeda monthly financial support with the expectation that her children finish school and not get pregnant. However, Cherlonda just didn't seem to appreciate that "children having children" makes for a tough start in life. I felt discouraged, and for a time we limited our interactions with the family. However, in the end we could not turn our backs on this young woman whom we had taken into our hearts.

After several difficult years raising two young kids, Cherlonda showed her resolve. She attended community college classes to get her high school diploma and then told us she wanted to be a chef. She had her eye on an executive chef degree from a renowned culinary college. It looked like a daunting task, given that it was a private college with expensive tuition. We were initially dismissive of what seemed like a pipe dream.

"We're willing to help you, but that's an expensive program," Deidre told her, encouraging her to consider more realistic options. However, Cherlonda was determined. She spent hours online, putting together a package of financial aid and grants and loans, until her shortfall was less than $3,000 a year. Impressed with what she had been able to cobble together, we agreed to cover the shortfall.

It was a difficult two years as she raised her two children, attended school, and tried to earn enough money to feed everyone. Fortunately, Cherlonda's mother was available to help with the kids, and they continued to live with her in her Habitat home. Upon graduation, Cherlonda faced an even more daunting task: securing employment that would provide enough money for her two children and to service her student loans. She eventually received a Section 8 housing voucher to move out of her mom's house with the kids, but she ended up in an unsafe neighborhood. Landlords who will accept Section 8 vouchers are few because of the nightmare of dealing with federal Department of Housing and Urban Development (HUD) inspections and other red tape.

Cherlonda wanted a safer neighborhood than the one she could afford. After several years of watching Cherlonda prove her commitment to working hard but still struggle to make ends meet, Deidre agreed to purchase a house in a nicer neighborhood and rent it to her. The HUD inspections that had to occur prior to her move-in took weeks to complete as the house sat empty. The agency required handicap railing on the stairs, for example, despite Cherlonda being a twenty-year-old without any physical handicap. Shortly after she moved in, HUD cut the voucher without warning, claiming that the house would be more expensive to maintain and that therefore she deserved less support. As later chapters will explain, many of HUD's policies often have been set up to penalize people who try to improve their lives. They do the opposite of what one would hope our government would do, which would be to encourage people to improve their contributions to society.

Despite the reduced voucher and the numerous obstacles, Cherlonda, with Deidre's assistance, set up a new home in a much safer neighborhood where her daughters had opportunities that would not be afforded to them otherwise. A positive, safe, and stable environment is vital to a child's mental growth and confidence. With the knowledge that her children were safe, Cherlonda also gained confidence, and her life took a dramatic turn for the better.

Today, she runs the catering department for a well-known national grocery chain. With Cherlonda as a role model—she earned the family's first associate degree—the rest of her family also has built steadily toward something better. B.J. works with her at the company. Unique recently graduated with a bachelor's degree, another first for their family, and she is committed to social work and giving back to others. She has also been accepted to graduate school. Their mom paid off her Habitat house and sold it for enough to purchase a nice townhouse—and her only two grandbabies seem like eager learners, ready for a promising future. Cherlonda is committed to teaching them the importance of not having children at such a young age and opening their eyes to other possibilities.

Cherlonda and her daughters are still very much a part of our lives. It is not unusual for us to have dinner with them when one of our kids is home, and Deidre makes it a point to visit with the daughters several times a month. Over the past two decades, they have spent several Christmas Days with us. My family has been honored to befriend Cherlonda's family and to have had the opportunity to influence and be influenced by them. We have seen firsthand how a decent home in a good community can put a family on track to prosperity.

AN ALIGNMENT OF VISION

Habitat for Humanity is an incredible organization. By promoting homeownership, it helps to stabilize neighborhoods. More importantly, it stabilizes families, who must maintain financial responsibility to hold on to their investment.

We have seen firsthand how a decent home in a good community can put a family on track to prosperity.

Habitat homes are not gifts; they are purchased by the families. In lieu of a down payment, a new homeowner must put in one hundred hours of work time as equity. That is generally spent working on somebody else's house, but you can get credit for working on your own house. You also must go through training on how to be a responsible homeowner and how to manage your finances. A family then buys its house at cost, with a fifteen- or twenty-year loan at zero interest.

Since building that first house in Belmont, my family has remained personally involved with Habitat for Humanity—in fact, my son Davis and I recently worked together on a Habitat construction site. Deidre was a volunteer for about a dozen years, serving on the board for nearly a decade and taking on various other volunteer roles, including chairperson of the family selection and family services committees. My brother formerly served as chairman of the Habitat board in Raleigh.

Grubb Properties has been involved in the construction of four Habitat houses through the years and recently finished its fifth. It was in Winston-Salem, North Carolina, an area where Grubb Properties got its early start but had not invested for thirty years before our most recent plans to build eight hundred apartments in the city's downtown. Our company has built houses in Raleigh, Lexington, and Charlotte, and also gave Habitat several lots in Lexington. Grubb Properties used to collect all the mortgage payments for Habitat of Charlotte, and during the global financial crisis we sold the organization several new homes that we had acquired in a challenged neighborhood as part of a larger package we purchased from a lender. Habitat purchased those houses for the amount that we had paid, without a markup—and for a fraction of the cost of building new Habitat homes.

The Habitat program lays the groundwork for success. It has made a big difference in hundreds of thousands of lives around the world. It has brought hope and progress to many neighborhoods.

Grubb Properties shares the philosophy that Habitat for Humanity has played a critical role in advancing. Our roots, too, are in providing help for first-time home buyers.

In our early days, virtually everyone who purchased a house from us had never owned one before. In fact, for many, no one in their families had ever taken that step. My father understood that homeowners take better care of their property and invest more in their communities. The reason is simple: They have some skin in the game. They feel empowered and energized by improving their lives and their surroundings. At Grubb Properties, we believe it is critical to enhance the communities we serve and the people who inhabit them. We must strive to lift people, not keep them down.

Homeowners take better care of their property and invest more in their communities.

Our society has far to go in that regard. Today countless folks cannot find an affordable home, whether to buy or to rent. Many feel trapped in poverty, unable to climb out. The situation is worsening. Habitat for Humanity, like Grubb Properties, is doing something about it, but we are only making a small dent in a problem that is accelerating daily.

THE GROWING DEMAND

Unfortunately, the struggles that Cherlonda's family faced in finding safe and affordable housing within a supportive community are not unusual today. The barriers can be significant to overcome with limited access to assistance. Important programs like Habitat for Humanity have a virtually endless demand but limited resources to meet it.

Making a difference must start with understanding just where we are today. Currently, we are facing the greatest housing affordability crisis since the end of World War II. Affordable housing in urban areas—where the best job, education, and economic mobility options are most plentiful—remains scarce while demand accelerates.

The millennial generation's demand for housing plays a major role in the worsening shortage. Born in the 1980s and 1990s, these young people began reaching adulthood in the 2000s, pouring into the workforce and looking for their first apartments. At 83.1 million people, they make up the largest generation of renters and prospective renters in US history. But with supply not keeping up, 22.8 million of them were still living at home with their parents or were in school as of 2017, according to the US Census Bureau.[3] In fact, more twenty-year-olds are living at home with their parents than at any time since the Great Depression of the 1930s. According to Pew Research Center, over one-third of all twenty-five- to twenty-nine-

---

3   Jonathan Vespa, "The Changing Economics and Demographics of Young Adulthood: 1975-2016," United States Census Bureau, April 2017, https://www.census.gov/library/publications/2017/demo/p20-579.html.

year-olds are still living with their parents.[4]

And there are still more to come. The peak year for births was 2007, and the children born around that time will be looking for their first apartments in the mid-2020s into the 2030s.

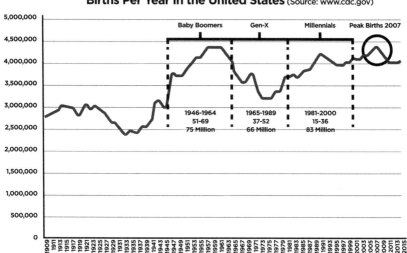

Births Per Year in the United States (Source: www.cdc.gov)

Harvard University's Joint Center for Housing Studies has projected that by 2025, the number of prospective renters is expected to be 47 million, up from 42.6 million in 2015.[5] In its 2017 annual report, the center reported solid growth was continuing in most rental markets, with the addition of 600,000 renter households in the previous year. That marked twelve consecutive years of growth, with 10 million new renters since 2005. The number of renting households is currently at a fifty-year high.

Many of those renters are not just millennials but their parents

4 Kristen Bialik and Richard Fry, "Millennial Life: How Young Adulthood Today Compares with Prior Generations," Pew Social Trends, Pew Research Center, February 14, 2019, https://www.pewsocialtrends.org/essay/millennial-life-how-young-adulthood-today-compares-with-prior-generations/.

5 "Projections & Implications for Housing a Growing Population: Older Households 2015-2035," Joint Center for Housing Studies, Harvard University, https://www.jchs.harvard.edu/sites/default/files/harvard_jchs_housing_growing_population_2016_1_0.pdf.

and grandparents as well. The baby boomers are joining the young folks in the search for scarce apartments in urban environments. The surge in rental demand that began in 2005 has been broad-based and includes many older adults who traditionally have been home-owners, the Harvard center pointed out in its 2017 report. In fact, people fifty-five and over accounted for 44 percent of the growth in renter households between 2005 and 2016. People under thirty-five accounted for 25 percent of the growth in the market, and this demand will accelerate as they form their own households.

Among other findings, the Harvard researchers reported that families with children have been increasingly likely to rent rather than buy a home. In 2016, 39 percent of those families were renting, a reflection of the many foreclosures during the housing crisis and a lingering reluctance to buy homes in the wake of the Great Recession.

The typical income for a renter household was just $37,900 in 2015, the study reported, and sixteen million renter households earned less than $25,000. Of those, eleven million were below the federal poverty level. Meanwhile, rents continue to increase rapidly in most markets. The Harvard report noted that the demand for affordable rental housing was increasingly high while the supply of such housing was diminishing.

The right kind of new development plays a critical role in addressing this affordability crisis. Investors and developers who care about the issue should look at ways to provide efficient and cost-effective apartments in urban communities to fill the void that luxury construction obviously fails to meet.

Grubb Properties seeks to fill that void with its Link Apartments brand. We look for efficiencies to drive down the rental price for a unit while providing the amenities that residents want. Most young folks are willing to trade overall square footage for a more affordable rent, especially in safe neighborhoods with accessible job opportunities. At Grubb Properties, we are highly focused on using just six floor plans throughout our Link Apartments portfolio in our attempts to make each building as efficient as possible. In 2007, a typical one-bedroom apartment averaged 850 square feet. Today, our largest one-bedroom unit is less than 600 square feet, and we have units with less than 400 square feet. We have found that a well-designed home more than satisfies our renters' needs and allows them to afford a place in a quality community.

THE DWINDLING SUPPLY

Our nation has not come close to adequately addressing the boom in housing demand. Construction of new multifamily rental units nationwide remains lower than during any decade in the past half century, according to US Census Bureau figures and the property data firm CoStar. The annual average between 1968 and 2016 was 397,000 new units. In the past decade, however, the growth has dipped as low as about 200,000 units a year. Construction has picked

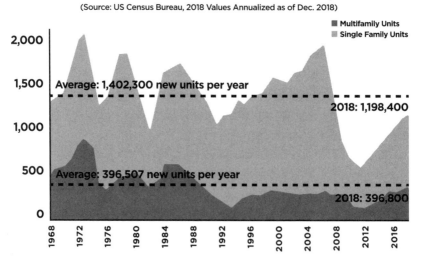

Total New Housing Construction (000's of Housing Units)
(Source: US Census Bureau, 2018 Values Annualized as of Dec. 2018)

■ Multifamily Units
■ Single Family Units

Average: 1,402,300 new units per year

2018: 1,198,400

Average: 396,507 new units per year

2018: 396,800

up, but most of these new homes are luxury developments at the very top of the market. Meanwhile, the country loses about 100,000 units each year to obsolescence. Given that the units lost are the least expensive, it is easy to see how the affordability crisis is worsening.

Between 2010 and 2016, the number of apartments that families with a very low income could afford fell by more than 60 percent nationwide, according to an October 2017 report by Freddie Mac, the government-backed mortgage financier.[6] A "very low income," the report explained, is less than half the median for a household in a given region. An affordable rent is considered to be no more than 30 percent of household income. For example, Charlotte's median household income for 2018 was $53,274, so a family earning half that, or $26,637 a year, could afford no more than $666 a month in rent.[7]

In most major metropolitan areas, the increase in rents has been outstripping income growth, David Brickman, the head of Freddie Mac Multifamily, told the *Washington Post*.[8] Rents went up as people who lost their homes in the housing crisis competed for the limited supply of apartments. In 2009, the apartment vacancy rate was 8 percent. By 2017, it was only 4 percent. The days are nearly over when a low-income family can afford an apartment without a government subsidy, Brickman said.

In seven of the nine states where Freddie Mac financed the most apartments, it found a significant drop in the percentage of units affordable to very-low-income families. The biggest gaps were in

---

6   Tracy Jan, "America's Affordable-Housing Stock Dropped by 60 Percent from 2010 to 2016," Washington Post, Oct. 23, 2017, https://www.washingtonpost.com/news/wonk/wp/2017/10/23/americas-affordable-housing-stock-dropped-by-60-percent-from-2010-to-2016/.

7   "Economy in Charlotte, North Carolina," Sperling's Best Places, accessed July 20, 2019, https://www.bestplaces.net/economy/city/north_carolina/charlotte.

8   Jan, "America's Affordable-Housing Stock."

Colorado and North Carolina. In Colorado, mostly in the Denver area, the number of affordable units dropped from 32 percent to 4 percent. In North Carolina, mostly in the Charlotte area, it dropped from 10 percent to 0.3—down to just a fraction of 1 percent. The other states seeing declines were Arizona, Georgia, Nevada, Texas, and Washington.

Most of the new multifamily housing construction has been catering to high-income renters, Freddie Mac reported. It's at the lower end of the market where the affordability issue is getting progressively severe. The Harvard researchers found that in 2008, the number of US households paying more than half their income on housing was 2.1 million. By 2014, that had risen to 11.4 million, and I heard a recent statistic at an Urban Institute gathering stating the number is over 19 million today.

An array of factors has been contributing to the sluggish supply of new affordable apartments. Primarily, a lack of capital has been available for construction, as lenders have been facing significant tightening in regulations. Also, the available labor has been in short supply. You can build only so many apartments if you lack the workers to do the job. A scarcity of workers has contributed to ever higher construction costs each year—and that, in turn, translates to less affordable rents.

Starting in 2013, the annual increase in construction costs topped 4 percent nationwide, rising to 5.6 percent during 2018, according to the Turner Construction Cost Index. That has outpaced the growth in both wages and the GDP. The index is based on labor rates and productivity, material prices, and the competitive condition of the marketplace. As 2019 began, further upward pressure on costs continued. The report cited shortages of skilled labor in a busy construction market.

SNAPSHOT OF AFFORDABLE HOUSING

CONSTRUCTION COST INCREASES

Year	Average Index Based on the 1967 base of 100	△%
2017	1038	5.0
2016	989	4.7
2015	943	4.5
2014	902	4.4
2013	864	4.1
2012	830	2.1
2011	812	1.6
2010	799	-4.0
2009	832	-8.4
2008	908	6.3
2007	854	7.7
2006	793	10.6
2005	717	9.5
Source: Turner Construction Cost Index		

Although many more people today are drawn to live in urban environments, developers find it tougher to build there. The cost of land is an obvious challenge, but there are other complications. Out in the suburbs, a developer can mow down thirty acres of trees and get a flat piece of land where crews can start throwing up two-by-fours. In the city, a builder's life gets much more complicated. As just one example, the cost to provide parking facilities for tenants is much higher in urban areas. Building an underground facility can cost as much as $50,000 per space, compared with less than $1,500 for a single surface parking space in the suburbs.

Overall, the average cost to build a new apartment in many cities in the United States is getting close to $250,000 per unit. Meanwhile, financing costs are increasing, and many developments are financed with short-term debt that makes them vulnerable to those increases. For a developer building an apartment community, every percentage point that the interest rate goes up means that an additional $100 must be added to the rent to produce the same return on investment. Let's say a developer builds a two-hundred-unit community costing $50 million, financed at 65 percent loan-to-cost. To cover a rate increase of just one percentage point, the developer would need to bring in $1,300 more per unit each year. So, up goes the rent. That's an unfortunate reality for folks hoping to afford an apartment in an area where they stand a chance of getting ahead.

The cost of developable land is usually the largest obstacle to creating new apartments in desirable locations accessible to neighborhood amenities and job centers. Land costs have soared over the past several years, more than tripling in price in many markets over the past decade. Finding quality development sites at a reasonable cost is the primary obstacle for any value-based development. Developers also face the challenge of the NIMBY syndrome, or "not in my backyard." As we have seen, many people believe that providing accommodations for people of lesser income will invite crime and drag down a neighborhood, so they set up barriers that further frustrate progress and add to the expenses.

It is possible to offset certain costs. For example, in our Link Apartments development in downtown Winston-Salem, North Carolina, we were able to secure numerous subsidies. In a joint venture with Wake Forest University, we secured an attractive land lease, a $6 million direct subsidy from the city, a five-year tax abatement under the state's Brownfields program, and long-term parking leases for daytime use of our deck when most residents are not home. Such creative approaches are essential in order to make affordable housing possible in areas with the greatest demand.

The government itself also can put up barriers. The shared parking deck I mentioned in Winston-Salem is a central component of our business model for affordable apartments. Setting up shared parking between office and apartment uses reduces expenses for building and parking operations. For example, a typical hundred-thousand-square-foot office building requires a 350-space parking deck, and a typical 280-unit apartment community also requires a 350-space parking deck. Combined, that is 700 structured parking spaces. However, the office folks' peak demand is in the daytime, and the apartment residents' peak demand is at night. If we put those uses next to each other and have them share one parking deck, we can get by providing only 480 structured parking spaces, which saves approximately $5 million in construction costs and creates a recurring savings of almost 40 percent for parking operations.

This is a critical component of our strategy to keep rents more affordable. However, HUD, one of the largest financing agencies for new apartment construction, has argued that people in the South don't go for that sort of thing. As a result, I know of two apartment projects that were denied HUD financing because they did not have dedicated separate parking. They also forced us to separate the parking on our latest HUD-financed deal, resulting in millions of dollars in unnecessary construction costs and making rental affordability harder to achieve.

It would seem HUD does not see affordable housing as part of its urban development mission. HUD has many dedicated employees with big hearts who are trying to do right, but often they too feel frustrated with an organization that is unable to adapt to today's realities, operating on inertia like a grinding wheel. Its policies often have kept people down and builders away. For years, it parceled people into slums and kept them there by capping what they could earn in order to get a subsidy, squelching their incentive to escape. Meanwhile, other policies have squelched developers' incentive to build the affordable communities where those folks might go. The bureaucratic inertia of HUD must be reformed if we want to put a dent in the housing crisis, a point that I will revisit later.

BUILDING HOMES, BUILDING LIVES

Rest assured that despite the startling statistics, it is possible to overcome this housing shortage. Many investors have remained gun-shy since the recessionary years that are now long past. Despite the demographics that point clearly to solid long-term opportunities, some still fear that the industry might cycle back to bust. Hesitating to put money into multifamily housing, they sideline the capital that could be put to good use for so many people. Even if an economic collapse were to send assets plunging broadly, I believe housing has one of the greatest margins of safety and would be one of the last investments that might lose money. Everyone needs a place to call home.

Consider again the realities of supply and demand, the bedrock of economics. When people need something badly and have trouble getting it, the price goes up. Only once the supply outstrips the demand will there be any relief in housing prices.

I believe housing has one of the greatest margins of safety and would be one of the last investments that might lose money.

Nonetheless, in the early years of the new millennium, developers were scrambling to build single-family houses despite the fact that the pool of first-time buyers was primarily from the "baby bust" that followed the baby boom. They were fewer than any generation in decades. Along with the fraud and greed that ultimately crashed the market, the industry had a fundamental problem. It was overbuilding at a time when there weren't many new household formations. Today, demand for housing is at a high, while building trends only represent about 50 percent of the level prior to the global financial crisis of 2008–09. As a result, housing prices have skyrocketed and more than 80 percent of the population cannot afford the average price of a newly built home, which reached $404,200 in August 2019, according to the US Census Bureau.[9]

Meanwhile, renters have been flooding into the housing market, looking for affordable living opportunities. They include the millennials and the boomers alike. They include folks like Cherlonda and her family who have a dream for a better life and deserve to live in a decent community where hope prevails over despair. This increasing demand has been going largely unmet. This is a demand that the industry, and the government, should be striving to fulfill. It's time for a brighter day.

---

9 "Median and Average Sales Prices of New Homes Sold in United States," United States Census Bureau, https://www.census.gov/construction/nrs/pdf/uspricemon.pdf.

CHAPTER 3

BACK ON TRACK

> *You build on failure. You use it as a steppingstone. Close the door on the past. You don't try to forget the mistakes, but you don't dwell on it. You don't let it have any of your energy, or any of your time, or any of your space.*
>
> **Johnny Cash**

"I AM SO DISAPPOINTED in you. I cannot believe you are ruining the character of Glen Lennox," my mother scolded me. I was shocked. Mom had passed several years earlier, after all, but it seemed as if she had come down from heaven to set me straight. The words sounded just like her.

"It just breaks my heart," the voice continued. Snapping back to reality, I saw that my critic was actually Mary Hill, who had pulled me aside after a meeting of the Environmental Defense Fund advisory board for North Carolina.

Mary lived near the Glen Lennox Apartments in Chapel Hill,

which Grubb Properties had managed since purchasing it in 1985, and she was fond of it. She wanted us to preserve its unique character as we planned a twenty-year redevelopment of the seventy-acre neighborhood—a project that we commenced in 2007. Mary's family had been a major benefactor to the University of North Carolina, and I respected her opinion.

This was during the frothy days of the real estate market just before it came tumbling down in 2008. Against my better judgment, I had acquiesced to some team members who envisioned a new Glen Lennox and had hired planners to redevelop it into a new urban style of neighborhood. I knew we would encounter resistance, but I dramatically underestimated the passion that the project would inflame.

The neighborhood went ballistic. Neighbors and residents began wearing "Save Glen Lennox" T-shirts. They launched a website called saveglenlennox.org. They filed for protection as a neighborhood conservation district (NCD). The neighbors were organized and furious.

Realizing that a fight would only make things worse for the Glen Lennox residents, the neighborhood, and us, I agreed not to appeal the NCD designation. I stood in front of the town council and apologized for our initial thoughtless plan. I formally withdrew our zoning application. I told the council I wanted to save Glen Lennox's character just like everyone else, but that did not necessarily require many of its obsolete buildings. I then agreed to become an active participant in the NCD process.

To facilitate a healthy discussion and plan, the town created a committee of approximately fifteen members. It agreed to give Grubb Properties three seats at the table, three seats to Glen Lennox residents, and three seats to the neighborhood members. The remainder of the seats went to elected officials, nonprofit stakeholders, and one of the commercial tenants. During the next five and a half years, Todd Williams, my right-hand person at Grubb Properties and also an architect and planner, along with Vanessa Blackwood-Spinks, the property manager of Glen Lennox, and I attended thirty-seven community meetings.

This was a public process with lots of media coverage and attention from people all over the state. The University of North Carolina's (UNC) Kenan-Flagler School of Business held a nationwide case competition using Glen Lennox as the challenge case. Business schools including UCLA, UC Berkeley, MIT, and others proposed plans for Glen Lennox's redevelopment. Todd ended up as one of the judges for that case competition.

In addition, UNC's planning school joined in the studies. The school's second-year planning students formed teams to create new master plans of Glen Lennox. I was unable to attend the teams' formal presentations, but I did get a chance later to have four of the teams present to me. The designs were highly creative, from large lake options to new urbanistic village settings. What amazed me, though, was that every team wiped out the character of Glen Lennox—and none kept the Glen Lennox name. I explained to the students how hard it is to create a brand identity and discussed the value I perceived in the Glen Lennox name and image, the importance of honoring history.

I realized we would need to dig deeper into the history and nature of this community to come up with a workable solution. What did the residents and people like Mary Hill mean by "saving" their community? What made it so special that they were willing to fight for it? What did they fear losing?

A CHAPEL HILL TRADITION

In the late 1940s, veterans returning from World War II were pouring into colleges across the nation on the GI Bill and creating an enormous demand for housing, particularly in college communities such as Chapel Hill. UNC enrollment increased by nearly 70 percent from 1941 to 1946. By 1950, the town's population was over 250 percent greater than it had been a decade earlier.

To address the severe housing shortage, the UNC president, W.D. Carmichael, collaborated with local contractor William Muirhead on a development modeled after the modern planned communities featured prominently in the magazines of the day. Muirhead consulted with architect Leif Valand to design Glen Lennox, which opened in 1950.

A Scotsman by heritage, Muirhead chose "Glen" as a tribute to the Highland valleys of his homeland and "Lennox" after his wife's maiden name. He got personal, as well, with the streets; for example, he named Hamilton Road after the street in Scotland where his wife grew up. The design incorporated wide, winding streets and sidewalks to accommodate cars and pedestrians alike.

In developing the tract, Muirhead preserved many of the trees and also planted new ones along the streets. He built 314 apartments in single-story brick buildings that looked like picturesque cottages with lawns and plantings. Within three years after the development opened, he built an additional 126 apartment homes.

Muirhead also envisioned a modern shopping center that would serve this new village and other Chapel Hill residents. The Glen Lennox Shopping Center was completed in 1952. The two-story structure, with a covered arcade supported on slender steel columns, included the Colonial Grocery Store, the Dairy Bar Restaurant, and a full-service Sinclair Gas Station. Nearby was plenty of free parking.

The shopping center also had a gift shop, laundromat, beauty salon, bank, and pharmacy, all of which would become local institutions. In fact, the original gift shop, Pace Gifts, would remain a part of Glen Lennox for over fifty years.

As the baby boomer generation arrived on the scene during the postwar years, Glen Lennox became a favorite among young families and graduate students. Muirhead provided shuttle buses to the campus but restricted undergraduates from renting, thereby giving the community a base of somewhat older residents who took pride in the neighborhood. Those graduate students went on to become some of the state's most notable lawyers, doctors, businesspeople, and politicians.

Glen Lennox and its shopping center were something fresh and exciting in the American experience. The postwar years were an era of optimism, with the promise of streamlined living and modern amenities. This was an ideal place to build a life—to launch a career, raise a family, and look back at the memories.

Throughout its history, Glen Lennox had low turnover among nonstudent residents. Once they moved in, folks tended to stay for a while, as did the owners and their managers. There have been only three owners in seven decades: Muirhead, the Kenan family, and Grubb Properties. What is more impressive is there have only been three property managers, starting with C.E. "Mac" McIntosh and ending with Vanessa, who has been the manager since 1985.

Looking at the roster of residents who have lived at Glen Lennox, it is a who's who of North Carolina. Choo Choo Justice, the most famous football player to come out of the University of North Carolina, lived there, as did Roy Williams, UNC's current basketball coach and one of only six coaches to win three NCAA Men's Division I national championships. It also included my father,

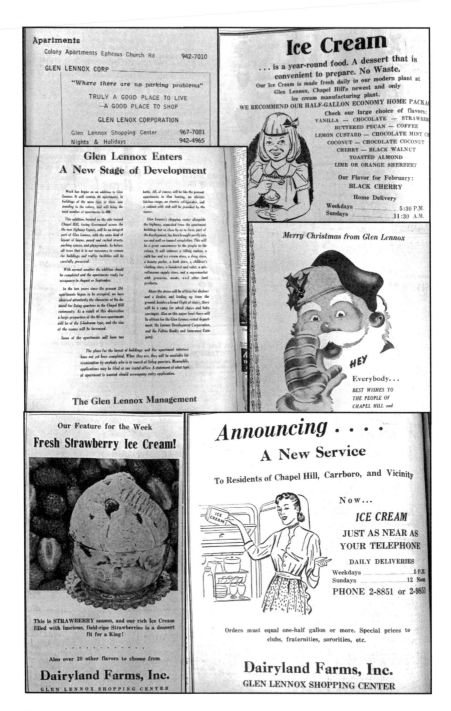

Postwar advertisements for Glen Lennox and its shopping center.

Robert Grubb, and the father and mother of Grubb Properties' chief financial officer, Henry Lomax. In fact, they birthed Henry while still living at Glen Lennox.

One of my favorite Glen Lennox stories came from a dinner I had with our attorney in Charlotte one night.

"I didn't know Grubb Properties owned Glen Lennox," Bailey Patrick said. "I loved Glen Lennox. I lived in three different addresses there, and Rose and I had two of our three children while living at Glen Lennox."

I asked him where he had lived in the development. "That was thirty-five years ago, my memory is not that good," he said, "but I do recall that one of those places was 11 Hamilton."

I smiled. "Really? Do you remember who was your next-door neighbor?"

"You have to be kidding—that was a long time ago," he said, but after some reflection he told me that he thought UNC's golf coach had lived next to him.

"Mr. Kinney?" I asked.

"Yeah, I think that was his name." He tilted his head. "How do you know that?"

"Because he still lives there!" I said with a laugh. "In fact, Mrs. Kinney is so sweet, she actually bakes a cake for the staff whenever they come to fix anything in her apartment." Unfortunately, the Kinneys are no longer with us, but they lived the remaining years of their lives at Glen Lennox.

As a result of its complementary mix of long-term residents and graduate students, the vacancy rate has been consistently very low; Glen Lennox remained at least 93 percent occupied even during the great overbuilding period of the late '80s and early '90s, and occupancy always spiked during times of financial crisis. This is primarily a result of its proximity to one of the top universities in the country and the demand for such a school when economic times are difficult. It is also a result of Glen Lennox's own modest rents when compared to newer communities. With its consistent and reliable revenue growth, Glen Lennox has proved to be a powerful investment.

A CLEAR MESSAGE

During the NCD process, we learned what the residents of Glen Lennox and the neighborhood loved the most. They weren't dead set against change, but they wanted it to be done the right way. During the dozens of discussions, we ultimately agreed upon eleven principles to guide the proposed redevelopment. Those principles were meant to preserve the most fundamental elements of Glen Lennox's character while allowing for improvements that would serve the neighborhood for decades to come. The principles are:

→ Value the history of the neighborhood and the Glen Lennox apartment and commercial property

→ Preserve the street network

→ Create and maintain public open space

→ Balance the new development with preservation of the trees and tree canopy

→ Keep a portion of the buildings

→ Transition and vary density and heights of the buildings

→ Provide landscaped buffers for sensitive neighbors

→ Preserve the Church of the Holy Family's visibility and accessibility

→ Create an effective transportation strategy

→ Encourage community sustainability

→ Encourage and support community diversity

The residents recognized that the sixty-year-old buildings had settling foundations, roof problems, and structural cracks. Obsolescence was a reality and many of the buildings would need to be replaced, but the residents wanted us to keep some of them—and the consensus was that the neighborhood would benefit from a blend of the old and the new, mixed throughout the property. We realized that the shopping center was an architectural icon: North Carolina's second oldest shopping center of that design style. We needed to respect the community's history and legacy and maintain the style and character of the buildings, not necessarily the old bricks and mortar. Nobody was feeling nostalgic about all the aging structures. Something else touched their hearts.

They treasured the curvy roads that meandered through the shaded community. They were far more intriguing than an orderly and boring grid of streets with predictable views. Much of the canopy of trees should stay, as well, because without those arching limbs, the neighborhood would seem barren. After six decades, however, some of those trees were not doing so well. The residents understood that trees would need to be pruned, maintained, and eventually replaced. They just didn't want us to go crazy with the chainsaws and bulldozers.

The message to us was clear: *We love the wooded charm and open spaces of our neighborhood.*

And we soon learned that a prime feature we must preserve was the nature of the people themselves. They asked us to encourage diversity in their community, with a variety of housing choices for people of all ages, backgrounds, income, and abilities.

Nobody should be pushed aside in the name of progress and modernization, they told us. If only people of means can afford to live in the neighborhood, they said, then the neighborhood as they know it is gone. Again, a clear message: *Don't drive away the very thing that makes us special. Give us a real community of real people living real lives.*

> **Nobody should be pushed aside in the name of progress and modernization.**

In other words, the people of Glen Lennox wanted more of what they already had. They wanted an affordable urban lifestyle in an interesting place that they could be proud to call home—and providing that, wherever we go, is what Grubb Properties has always been about. I'm sure my mother would approve of how we are treating the good folks of Glen Lennox and the efforts we are putting into preserving its character.

GOODBYE TO THE CAR CULTURE

As we moved forward on a plan for Glen Lennox, we focused on what we had learned about what makes the community special. In designing a new clubhouse, for example, we reflected the look of the

A rendering of the new Glen Lennox clubhouse.

1950s shopping center, from the architecture down to the furniture styles. The new Glen Lennox logo celebrates the community's roots in that decade. The 1950s was a decade of cutting-edge design that reflected the perception that society was at the dawn of a bright new day. That has been our desire for Glen Lennox—to proudly honor its history as part of its future.

The car culture of the 1950s, however, is one aspect of that decade that we would rather leave behind. The society of the future will not necessarily be centered on the automobile. Time is precious, and commuters have had their fill of sitting in traffic jams on the highway every morning and afternoon. They want to live where they can walk or bike to work and to restaurants, shops, and entertainment. They want easy access to mass transit. Progressive developers are paying attention to that trend. At Glen Lennox, residents told us they wanted dedicated bike paths, plenty of sidewalks, and good bus service.

In the fall of 2017, I got the opportunity to visit Copenhagen, Denmark, with the Knight Foundation to experience the best in bicycle infrastructure. Nearly three-quarters of the residents in that nation's capital commute by bike. The majority of them do so because it is faster. I realized how much we could reduce costs for urban housing and other developments if we didn't have to park so many cars. Not to mention, there would be a dramatic improvement in health and overall quality of life.

The trip to Copenhagen inspired me to set an audacious goal for Glen Lennox. My vision is that by 2030, over 50 percent of all inbound and outbound commutes for Glen Lennox will be in some form other than automobile. In order to further this goal, we have hired Copenhagenize, a design group based in Copenhagen with a singular focus on the best bike design infrastructure. With them we are revisiting the design of our interchanges, our road layouts, and even our bike parking and cycle centers. With their help, we are also pushing the town of Chapel Hill to improve bike connectivity and expand their greenways.

Reducing dependency on the automobile can go a long way toward making housing more affordable.

Reducing dependency on the automobile can go a long way toward making housing more affordable. Buying and maintaining a car is expensive for the owner, but developers too have come to appreciate how expensive it is to accommodate cars by providing parking facilities. To construct an above-ground deck in an urban environment costs about $20,000 per parking space. A podium parking space under a building, but above ground, costs about $35,000 per space. Below ground, a parking space could cost 50 percent more than that. These costs are significant hurdles to providing affordable urban housing. If housing developers could save on the expense of building and maintaining parking facilities, they could offer apartments that rent for less. This thinking is part of what prompted our strategy of sharing parking spaces between multifamily and office uses.

Unfortunately, HUD has yet to understand the relationship between parking and affordable urban development. HUD, which financed our first apartment community at Glen Lennox, has insisted that the apartments have dedicated parking that is not shared with office users or others that work and live in a community. As a result, we have to build hundreds of additional parking spaces not required by the town of Chapel Hill nor desired by the community. This is adding over $2 million in additional cost to our apartment community, meaning we will need to charge approximately $1,400 more in rent for each apartment annually just to cover this unnecessary expense. It is this type of bureaucratic institutional thinking, which we will explore further in chapter five, that keeps so many people from realizing the urban dream.

TRUE COMMUNITY

As I write these words, Grubb Properties is still in the early stages of the Glen Lennox project, but the result of years of listening and incorporating many great ideas from the neighbors is resulting in a much greater asset for the community and for Grubb Properties. The mood in the community now feels welcoming, with excitement about what's to come versus the hostility we faced in 2007. We have submitted a twenty-year vision that will keep some of the existing apartments while gradually developing the site to add more housing along with office and retail space. Our aim is to bring jobs and better amenities to the people, right on site, where they can walk to work and entertainment options, while keeping a mixture of housing types throughout the property.

It was our reassurance and willingness to pay close attention to the people that turned the neighborhood's irritation into enthusiasm. The town sees us as a model developer—and Chapel Hill is not generally what you would call a prodevelopment town. Many builders have stayed away for fear that they will spend a lot of time and money on project design and planning but still be denied a permit, a situation that can devastate a real estate development company.

What my colleagues and I have experienced at Glen Lennox is the spirit of true community. The residents and town officials care deeply about the neighborhood. They are intent on preserving the best of it while also providing for the needs of upcoming generations. They are proud of their history, but they recognize that tomorrow will be part of their history too.

Glen Lennox is an example of what can go right when we all work together. People want to be heard. The government and the housing industry must listen with respect to the solutions they offer. Good ideas arise from the people who live and work and raise families in the communities we serve. We want them to stay—in fact, the Glen Lennox experience led to our policy that limits rent increases for all our long-term residents. Today, throughout our portfolio, we cap the rental increases to the Consumer Price Index for all residents who have lived with us for at least five years.[10] This program allows us to save turnover costs, but more importantly, it allows residents peace of mind that their homes will remain affordable. And in turn, it helps create authentic community, something everyone appreciates.

The people of Glen Lennox are a cross section of society— laborers, office workers, students, immigrants, and retirees. You can hear many languages spoken there. Some residents are relatively wealthy, and some need to count their pennies. They celebrate, they struggle, they endure, and through it all they share their lives as neighbors and friends. That's the meaning of true community. Glen Lennox has it—and we are determined to help hold on to it.

THE IMPORTANCE OF PROCESS

Intently listening is how our company got back on track at Glen Lennox, and that's what the housing industry and the government must do to deal effectively with the coming crisis. In any industry,

---

10   Participation in this program is also capped at 15 percent of the total rental units in a community.

a prosperous business tunes in to people's needs and finds creative ways to fulfill them. Any government that is doing its job should be looking out for the interests of all its citizens. I was recently working with the McColl Center for Visual Arts in Charlotte to assist with the challenging gentrification issues that will sweep through its neighborhood, and its approach was that the process is often more important than the outcome.

A tidal wave of new renters is sweeping in, and they deserve quality living spaces near employment opportunities and other community amenities. We need to figure out how to overcome the "not in my backyard" syndrome that paralyzes so many neighborhoods. We need to have serious dialogue and conversations to build trust. A process where developers parachute in to check off a box with a single neighborhood meeting often erodes trust. It takes true engagement to build trust with a neighborhood, as no one can understand the true issues or concerns in a single meeting or two.

Much of today's housing problems stem from the insidious spirit of segregation. It has done untold damage to our country and persisted beyond the Jim Crow laws that were a way of life from the Civil War to the civil rights era. Segregation continued in the North as African Americans migrated en masse from the South. For decades, the government lumped the poorest of the poor together into public housing projects, another manifestation of segregation.

What that "urban renewal" got us was block after block of poverty and desolation: Cabrini-Green in Chicago, Pruitt-Igoe in St. Louis, Jordan Downs in the Watts district of Los Angeles, and many others. All of them are, or were, dangerous places, wracked with crime. People need to understand that what they see in these places has nothing to do with skin color or ethnicity. Desperate people will act desperately when stacked together with other desperate people in high-rise hells where there seems no cause for hope. We should have expected something better from our policymakers of every stripe.

According to urban studies theorist Richard Florida, by 2009, more than 85 percent of the residents of America's cities and metro areas lived in locations that were more economically segregated than they were in 1970. The share of American families living in either all-poor or all-rich neighborhoods more than doubled during that same period. However, he goes on to say in his book *The New Urban Crisis* (2017) that the prospects for upward economic mobility are greatest in urban areas so long as poor and working-class people are not forced out by rising housing costs. In less populated areas where the disadvantaged live farther from jobs and opportunities, Florida says, economic mobility is substantially hampered.

There is hope. Across the nation, for example, HUD's Hope VI program has made strides in turning around the mistakes of the past, replacing blight with attractive and affordable housing in diversified communities. In the First Ward of downtown Charlotte, the program has changed lives. The First Ward once had the city's highest murder rate. Hundreds of poor families still live there, but today it is a place where folks of mixed cultures and incomes are neighbors and friends. The mayor at the time, Anthony Foxx, lived there for years until he became US secretary of transportation. So did Wells Fargo economist Mark Vitner. Our son, Davis, went to school in the First Ward through the eighth grade. One day a month, kids in his class would walk to the nearby homeless shelter to play soccer with the people staying there and to do arts and crafts with them—along with other service outreach projects. The First Ward is working.

In many communities across the nation, good things clearly have been happening. We need more of those good things. The housing industry and the government have a long way to go in providing affordable rentals in healthy, thriving neighborhoods, but the stories of success show that we can get there.

Let there be no doubt: The demand for that type of housing will be insatiable in the coming years. The demographics are clear. We will need a concerted effort by the private sector and all levels of government to avoid one of the greatest housing affordability crises since the 1930s. Those in positions of influence need to stop and listen, as my colleagues and I listened at Glen Lennox. The folks who deal with the daily issues, trying each day to make ends meet, deserve to be heard. Their voices can make a substantial difference as together we develop policies and build incentives for long-term prosperity and economic mobility for all. Our great democracy was created to give voice to the people; let's do what our founding fathers drafted in the Declaration of Independence and give them a chance to be heard.

> **We will need a concerted effort by the private sector and all levels of government to avoid one of the greatest housing affordability crises since the 1930s.**

CHAPTER 4

GETTING IT TOGETHER

> *A company's ability to weather storms depends very much on how seriously executives take their risk management function when the sun is shining and no clouds are on the horizon.*

Robert S. Kaplan and Anette Mikes

"IS IT SAFE FOR my only child to move back into the Link Apartments?" the worried mom implored, breaking into tears as she spoke to me. "How do I know it's safe?" Her daughter was a resident of our Link Apartments Glenwood South in downtown Raleigh,

North Carolina, across the street from the site of a fire on March 16, 2017, that was described as the city's worst in a century. The heat melted the entire side of our building. But thanks to round-the-clock work from our construction and property management teams, we were ready only two weeks later for most of the residents to come back home.

I could understand the mom's concerns. The images from that night were still fresh in everyone's minds, but our safety systems had been put to the test that night and they had worked flawlessly. Trying to reassure the mother, I said, "I don't know of another fire safety system that has been tested in real action the way ours was that night. I cannot offer any guarantees of safety, but I am confident that the chances of someone getting hurt by another fire in our building are lower than in 99 percent of the homes in America." Still, I reassured them both that Grubb Properties would respect her decision, whether it was to move back into her apartment or to end the lease and move elsewhere. We didn't want to force anyone to live where they were not comfortable.

As the mother continued to worry and push her daughter to choose to live elsewhere, the young lady finally spoke up. "Mom, that is my home." After her daughter defended the team and how they deserved her support, the mother acquiesced with tears of pride and love. She agreed that indeed the right decision was for her daughter to stay.

On the Monday following the fire, we reimbursed every resident the two weeks of rent they had paid for the remainder of March. We offered every resident the opportunity to cancel their lease without penalty, and we decided to offer a rent discount to those who decided to stay. In exactly fourteen days, we secured the city's approval to move folks back in—and virtually all those residents who were not already looking to move for another reason chose to come back. Fifty-nine apartments—the ones closest to the fire, about a quarter of the building—would need a year's worth of repairs and renovations before reopening, but we invited those people to move into whatever vacant units were available.

The fire had broken out shortly after ten o'clock that cold winter night and raced through the exposed wood framing of an apartment construction site across the street from our building. At that early stage of construction, no sprinkler system had been installed yet. The flames quickly roared higher than the adjacent seventeen-story Quorum Center office and condominium high-rise.

The intense heat eventually melted the base of a huge tower crane on the site. As the crane began to wobble, its base gave way. It began to fall toward the Link Apartments, but it twisted at the base and crashed through the roof of our adjacent property, an old one-story building less than twenty-five feet away—a building that housed the 911 response and Homeland Security services for all of downtown Raleigh. The crash sent the rooftop HVAC unit through the floor below, and all power in the block was cut off. During the fire, with temperatures hot enough to melt nearby windows and doors, a brave crew was able to get generators to the building within hours to restore Raleigh's critical emergency response systems.

The heat melted every door and window facing the blaze in the third, fourth, fifth, and sixth floors of our apartment building. At the seventeen-story Quorum building, some of the windows shattered instead of melting, and the falling glass struck a firefighter. It was the night's only reported injury, and he recovered. The fact that no one was killed was astonishing.

The cause of the fire was never determined, despite the best efforts by personnel from local and state organizations as well as the

FBI and ATF, who interviewed hundreds of people. The authorities removed tons of debris for examination.

As the sun rose Friday morning, mere hours after the flames had been extinguished, we got our first real look at the east side of our building. The side was scorched black, and all the upper-floor windows were melted—but the lower floor had suffered little damage, given that heat rises. On the inside of the building, window frames and door frames were hardly recognizable. In some places you could not see that glass had ever been installed. On the floor were the twisted remains of Venetian blinds. The fire damage generally extended only a few feet in from the windows, except in the units where the entire living room walls had been glass. In those few apartments, the damage extended about fifteen feet inside the home. As I toured the property, I was surprised to find wedding photos and stereo equipment perfectly intact, damaged only by sprinkler water, just three feet from window openings. Our fire safety system had worked even better than I could have hoped.

Despite that success, I was pretty sure we still would have smoke damage throughout the building that would be nearly impossible to repair. But to my surprise, the fire doors had closed and the remainder of the building didn't have the faintest scent of smoke. I was impressed with how well the system had performed. As a former president of the Charlotte Apartment Association, I often had preached about the success of sprinkler systems, proven to prevent injuries, but dealing with a fire this massive was new to me.

Our national disaster response contractor was on the scene by 4 a.m. Friday with a number of our team members, and they swept into action. By sunrise they were already removing trash bins of damaged wall materials and doing whatever was necessary to get folks back home as soon as possible.

The night of the fire was a cold one; the temperature was in the twenties as residents fled into the streets. Some stayed at hotels, some with family or friends. Many of our team members worked forty-eight straight hours, with the primary goal of helping residents secure their pets, their car keys, and other valuables and eventually get back into their homes.

The shift changes of fire and police chiefs were particularly painful. This is where my opinion of the chiefs starts to differ from how I feel about the hardworking people who make up the forces. In America, we have made the fire chief king in our zeal for safety. In many municipalities, the fire chief exercises that power with too much gusto, to the detriment of housing affordability.

In this instance, fortunately the fire chief on duty recognized the value of salvaging the building quickly. We mobilized close to 200 folks to start the process from our emergency response provider. But when that fire chief's shift was over, his replacement exercised his power and overruled the previous fire chief, forcing an evacuation. For hours, we had hundreds of employees on overtime sitting outside the building, many leaving to get some sleep—and then the chief on the next shift let them back in again once he was again convinced of the merits of moving quickly. The following day, the police chief decided to pull rank on the fire chief, forcing an evacuation of the entire block, including the building.

It was an embarrassing power struggle. Fortunately, we had a strong relationship with the city, and the city manager stepped in to coordinate communication between the fire and police departments so that our team could remain on the site to continue salvaging the building.

We had our first inspection the following Friday in an attempt to allow the more than 150 residents whose apartments had not been damaged to move back into their homes. At this point, our residents were scattered throughout the state. We learned that afternoon that we could not reopen until we replaced the fire system in every stairwell in the building, even those that were not damaged.

It was another example of what I believe was an overzealous fire chief; however, if you are in the building business, you know instinctively that when a fire chief asks you to jump, you ask, "How high?" To get on the wrong side of a fire chief or a building inspector can quickly spiral into countless delays, and I know of examples that have cost millions of dollars. Every prudent developer keeps a contingency amount of money to deal with such situations, because many inspectors don't care what was approved, and almost none interpret the code the same way. What one inspector makes us do, the next inspector might make us undo.

So instead of questioning why we were replacing perfectly good, if not almost brand new, fire alarms on the side of the building that was untouched, we called the system's manufacturer in Pennsylvania immediately to ship the parts. The company was closing for the weekend, however, and we were told the shipment would have to wait until the following week. Rob Duguid, our vice president of construction, convinced one of the employees to meet him the next morning with the systems. He drove through the night, over ten hours, to pick up the sensor equipment on Saturday morning and bring it back to Raleigh that same day, saving us a significant delay.

Thanks to the dedication of dozens of Grubb Properties' team members, we were able to move 156 individuals back into their apartments the following week. Raleigh officials told us that they never had seen a company as responsive. They were amazed to be able to approve our building's reopening so soon after "the fire of the century," as people were calling it. By contrast, nobody was moved back into the nearby Quorum condominiums for close to two years after the fire.

Our residents, too, were impressed with our quick action. All of them were relatively new, since the building had opened just the previous year. They already were pleased with us before the fire. In fact, just a day earlier, *Multifamily Executive* magazine had published its national list of top apartments based on online ratings and reviews. Link Apartments Glenwood South ranked number thirty-two out of sixty thousand apartment communities surveyed.

In the aftermath of the fire, we stood proud of ourselves, our residents, and our community. Together, we were "Link Strong," as we pronounced on a banner across the parking garage as folks came back home. The several million dollars in damage to our building was nothing compared to what might have been. We owe so much to the fortitude of the firefighters, more than a hundred strong, who tamed the flames and worked doggedly to keep the fire from spreading. They and the other first responders did more than protect property; they saved lives that night.

Heroes have many faces. After the fire, Grubb Properties donated to the Two Hundred Club of Wake County, which helps families of law enforcement and rescue personnel who have died in the line of duty. The bravery of these workers, time and again, averts catastrophe. They are the obvious heroes, but the lifesavers also include those who design and make the equipment that keeps our buildings safe and those who adopt and enforce the regulations that protect lives and livelihoods. It's because of all those folks that a worried mom was able to be reassured that, yes, her daughter would be just fine coming home.

A CULTURE OF COOPERATION

Challenging times are inevitable. It is how you prepare for them and respond during them that makes the difference. Prepared organizations establish routines. "They make exhaustive lists of things that could go wrong, they precheck them, and then every time they have an unexpected failure, they expand the list," Adam Grant, an organizational psychologist, author, and professor at the Wharton School of the University of Pennsylvania, told a Harvard Business Review reporter.[11] He is the coauthor, with Facebook executive Sheryl Sandberg, of *Option B: Facing Adversity, Building Resilience, and Finding Joy.*

By preparing themselves for an array of contingencies, the best organizations can quickly pull together with others and work cooperatively in times of crisis.

By preparing themselves for an array of contingencies, the best organizations can quickly pull together with others and work cooperatively in times of crisis. The Raleigh fire was just such a time. Though we could not have known it was coming, we understand that events like this happen, so we had comprehensive insurance, we had a national disaster response contract, and we had performed fire drills. We are committed to being prepared. So was the greater community—the city officials, the first responders, the inspectors, and all the others who worked together seamlessly. We feel fortunate that our tenants were safe and that our property could be restored to full occupancy.

Sometimes I think we have seen it all, though I know better than to make such a proclamation. It seems something new appears

---

11   Adi Ignatius, "Above All, Acknowledge the Pain," *Harvard Business Review*, May 2017, https://hbr.org/2017/05/above-all-acknowledge-the-pain.

every year. In 2016, Hurricane Matthew, which caused billions of dollars in damage in the coastal areas of Georgia and the Carolinas, wiped out half of an apartment community we own in Savannah. It was a major challenge, but when the sun came out, our staff set up grills and cooked hotdogs and hamburgers for anyone who was still around, which immediately lifted everyone's spirits.

Disasters can come in many forms. One that we faced recently was the result of our legislature's passing of House Bill 2, known as "the bathroom bill," requiring residents to use restrooms in public buildings that corresponded to their sex at birth. The bill had the effect of halting all corporate expansions to North Carolina and grinding job growth to a standstill. That was extremely painful for our office division and eventually began to hurt demand for apartments. In addition, my second-largest investor redlined investing in North Carolina, and we were forced to shift our growth elsewhere. The bill was eventually repealed, but by then our investors had suffered millions of dollars in damage due to lost revenue.

In other instances, we have had to remediate radon in the upper floors of a building. The radon was being emitted by the concrete used to construct the building, rather than coming from the ground as typically would be the case. Upon discovering the issue, we immediately notified all residents and then spent close to $2 million creating a solution to protect their health. We also had the unfortunate experience of having to vacate an entire apartment community of over 140 units due to a pest infestation that we could not get under control while the community was inhabited. Not to mention the events of 9/11—the same morning that we happened to hold the grand opening for a luxury townhome community. That same week, we also were to close on what would have been our largest development to date, a $50 million mixed-use joint venture, when the primary investor, while walking to his office, was hit by debris from the plane crash into the World Trade Center and hospitalized. Fortunately, he was released from the hospital after a couple of days without any long-term damage and closed with us on our investment a month later.

We have seen some incredible things in our times, and we know we haven't seen it all. At Grubb Properties, we continue to be optimistic and to focus on preparing for the next challenge, making sure we can avoid injuries and minimize damage without compromising anyone's health and safety. As a result, we have long been adding to our extensive "what to do" list for a wide variety of situations, and it starts with due diligence before we even acquire a property.

Crisis management is critical to any business model.

Crisis management is critical to any business model. Being caught unprepared can be lethal to residents and investors. We know we must deal with catastrophes head-on. Overcoming the Raleigh fire so quickly took determination, cooperation, and preparation, including the creation of a crisis management plan. That kind of reaction rarely happens without a high level of trust. Trust is built over time.

At Grubb Properties, we spend a lot of time thinking and talking about potential issues and building safety nets into our projections. Not only is it important to be prepared for unexpected events, but we all must recognize that there are real risks and costs to creating new housing. Development of new housing is risky. Solving the housing affordability crisis will require the support and cooperation of many.

It is critical that municipalities as well as companies prepare for natural disasters and respond efficiently. Failure to do so leads to ever more regulations, which often don't deal with the issue at hand. For example, in North Carolina, whenever someone dies in a fire, it feels like the response is always additional regulations for new housing developments. However, those fatalities happen in older apartment communities without sprinkler systems. As of the writing of this book, I am unaware of a single fatality or even a finger burn in a new apartment building in North Carolina with a sprinkler system. Despite that fact, fire departments typically will request additional protection over and above a sprinkler system, making housing less affordable. While safety is something that should not be compromised, these types of reactions contribute to making housing even less obtainable for Americans.

BIRTH OF A NEIGHBORHOOD

Grubb Properties has never been accused of lacking creativity. We have a can-do spirit and thrive when presented with a problem. However, the housing affordability crisis facing America is much bigger than us. Since we can't fix the problem nationwide, what we can do is shine a spotlight on opportunities. As a result, we have created fifty-eight levers that we pull to drive down the cost of building and operating urban developments.

In every project we develop, we use many combinations of those levers that we have identified to promote affordability. In a recent example, we found many such opportunities that together allowed us to reduce rents by $250 per month for incoming residents without compromising the quality of the community.

One of the most powerful levers is being demonstrated in our Montford Park project along the Park Road corridor of Charlotte. As a result of a lot of effort on the part of many entrepreneurs, this neighborhood will become the city's next hip district.

In October 2014, we purchased the old IBM office building

at 4601 Park Road. I was hesitant about the acquisition because the building felt obsolete—or, in my terms, it was seriously ugly. However, I liked the location, and as any real estate investor knows, the three main rules of real estate are location, location, and location.

The building was just a block from Montford Drive, long known for its bars and restaurants and for a circa-1958 bowling alley. For about a decade, a thriving nightlife scene had been developing on Montford Drive. Recently, the bowling alley had been significantly upgraded into an attractive anchor for the street, and one of Charlotte's top restaurants had landed on the street. In addition, city officials decided to extend the Little Sugar Creek greenway by the property. We felt that the vicinity was ripe for young professionals to also live and work there. When the adjacent building, a ten-story and arguably even uglier building, came available for sale, we purchased it, pulling together an entire block of more than ten acres.

Early on, we recognized the need to give this growing community an identity of its own, as opposed to it just being known as a stretch of Park Road south of Montford. In a creative move, my team decided to create an advisory group of neighborhood representatives and business owners. After much debate about branding ideas, we launched an online survey. The participation was astonishing. After more than six hundred neighbors chimed in with ideas, the consensus was "Montford Park." And a new neighborhood was christened.

Logo for the Montford Park neighborhood.

As a result of our success, other developers have jumped on the bandwagon and, to date, over one thousand apartments are planned or under construction in Montford Park. In addition, we now have restaurants and bars spilling off Montford throughout the Montford Park neighborhood. It can take decades for a neighborhood to evolve, but here it was happening so swiftly.

We wanted to add to this growing neighborhood, and along with our renovated office buildings, we saw an opportunity in the sea of parking lots surrounding these buildings. The acres of blighted asphalt were a deterrent to foot traffic to and from Montford Drive. The asphalt would exacerbate summer temperatures as the heat sweltered from the dark gaseous lot, and when it rained the dirty water would run off into the Little Sugar Creek, which was regaining its active uses thanks to the greenway. Our plans called for the creation of structured parking, new stormwater management, and over five hundred new apartments under the Link Apartments brand along the rear of our office buildings and a mixed-use project along Park Road.

Replacing the environmental nightmare of a parking lot with active uses improved the neighborhood and was a big win for more value-based housing. The rezoning allowed us to get apartment land for free, compared with the $11 million recently paid for the parcel designed for 285 apartments directly across the street. To be profitable, that project likely would need rents approaching $2,000 per month, while we could obtain a similar profit margin with rents averaging less than $1,400 a month. In addition, our parking decks would be shared between the office buildings and the new apartment community. As a result, the office buildings covered half the parking costs and also contributed a tremendous amount toward the recurring operating costs for the decks. These synergies not only play a significant role in our ability to keep rents affordable but also dramatically enhance the quality of the experience for the office user who now has covered parking next to their building and some of the workforce walking a few feet to work.

Since the cost of land, being the single largest up-front cost, is a major factor in the total cost of a project and, ultimately, in the amount of rent charged, our approach to converting office parking lots into housing goes far to promote affordability. In such instances, our office division gives us a significant competitive advantage in reaching a price point that renters can afford, and it provides us the ability to be patient when seeking entitlements to build the housing.

Since most municipalities are struggling with housing that will allow their middle class to evolve and prosper in their urban areas, they want us to keep those rents as low as possible and are more accommodating with entitlements and other zoning requests. We have also found more and more municipalities are willing to provide direct subsidies as well in return for caps on the income a percentage of our renters can earn.

While 75 percent of all new apartments being developed have starting rents that are only affordable to households earning salaries well in excess of the median income,[12] in our Link Apartments we have turned the art of apartment design into a science, with six superefficient floor plans that give residents the most for their money. Two of these floor plans are affordable for folks making as little as 60 percent of the median income. In most instances, over 90 percent of our apartments are affordable to households making below 100 percent of median income. I am proud that Link Apartments is able to fill a void found in most new urban developments and as a result

---

12   Laura Kusisto, "Luxury Apartment Boom Looks Set to Fizzle in 2017," *Wall Street Journal*, January 2, 2017, https://www.wsj.com/articles/luxury-apartment-boom-looks-set-to-fizzle-in-2017-1483358401.

will play an important role in assisting struggling households trying to improve their economic well-being.

IN IT FOR THE LONG HAUL

As we have continued to grow over the last half century, we have stayed well-grounded in what works. We focus on the essentials like location. We never make an investment in real estate we don't want to keep for a decade or longer. Inevitably, trying to make a quick buck turns into a long headache. When we focus on the long haul, good things happen, often to our surprise.

When we focus on the long haul, good things happen, often to our surprise.

A lot of apartment developers lean on short-term debt. Most are merchant builders who care mostly about their up-front costs, figuring that they soon will be selling to someone else who can worry about the recurring costs. Our vision goes beyond that. We had a ten-year construction/permanent loan on Link Apartments Glenwood South. Imagine our situation if we had short-term financing that expired shortly after we suffered the damage from Raleigh's largest fire in over a century. We would have been greatly distracted by lender issues that could have resulted in the potential of us losing our entire investment. The longer commitment meant our interests were aligned with our lenders, and they could not have been more grateful for our response to the disaster.

Focusing on the long term keeps our interests aligned with our residents' interests, too. Knowing that we will have a continuing responsibility for maintaining our properties, we naturally will be inclined to upgrade the building systems to protect our investment. Over time, that benefits both us and those who rent from us. What we save on future, recurring expenses helps us to keep our apartments affordable. In addition, our buildings all meet strict standards for sustainability, which also increases affordability by driving down utility costs for our residents. And we know that it helps to have residents who stay with us for the long term. That not only reduces the cost of turnovers and vacancies but improves our communities; folks take pride in neighborhoods that they have long called home. Our rent caps for five-year-and-beyond residents are among the ways that we encourage them to maintain their homes in our communities.

Grubb Properties strives to instill that lasting sense of community among residents. Our Link Apartments address one aspect of the housing affordability crisis by providing high-quality and convenient apartments at a reasonable price in urbanizing communities. Location matters not only for real estate investors but for those seeking economic mobility. Urban environments provide access to jobs, entertainment, and social capital.

As I write this, construction costs have risen more than 50 percent in five years. Land prices have increased dramatically, and interest rates are rising. The consequence is that developers can't deliver affordable housing products in our urban areas. Therefore, they are chasing the upper-income renter or condominium buyer. At Grubb Properties, we have decided to avoid the crowded upper-income market, an area where we have demonstrated great expertise, to focus our energies on helping improve economic mobility and housing affordability in the urban markets in which we operate.

WORKING TOGETHER

"Working together" are the first two words of Grubb Properties' vision. Providing affordable apartments to meet the surge in demand is not an easy undertaking. To make a dent in meeting that demand, our team has committed to working with the national government, municipal governments, and investors to help minimize the impact of today's crisis tomorrow.

In this book we have been examining a variety of ways that the industry can help to turn this crisis around. In the next three chapters, I discuss the role that each of those other three stakeholders has been playing, and could be playing, to provide many more people with desirable and affordable housing. We realize that change is not easy and that we will never get everyone working on the same priorities, but if we can shine a bright light on areas for improvement, we can change the lives of millions of Americans. It is time for all the players—industry, local and federal officials, and investors—to steadily improve the prospects for affordable rental housing. If we can get it together, we can all win.

CHAPTER 5

HELP FROM HIGH PLACES

> *You never change things by fighting the existing reality. To change something, build a new model that makes the existing model obsolete.*
>
> ### Buckminster Fuller

IT WAS MY WIFE, Deidre, who suggested that I check out the Seigle Avenue Presbyterian Church in the struggling Belmont neighborhood near uptown Charlotte. "I think you'd like it, Clay," she said, and I've learned through the years that I should pay attention when Deidre tells me something. "A lot of the people from Habitat go there. It sounds like your kind of place." It was. There I found an integrated congregation led by Charlie Summers, who delivered traditional services, but it was the choir led by Smitty Flynn that sold me. Having gone to school in New Orleans, I felt as if I were back in the Big Easy with even better gospel than I remembered.

Sometimes these days, as I play tennis with Davis or Rosalie on the Seigle Avenue courts near the restored greenway along Little

Sugar Creek, I glance up at the Charlotte skyline and think back on my nearly two decades of involvement in this long-challenged neighborhood. This was where Deidre and I participated in our first Habitat project—a house being constructed by Judy and Paul Leonard. Deidre had met Judy at Queens University, and Paul would go on to become chairman of Habitat International and eventually its president. This was also where we first met Cherlonda and her family, who lived directly across Allen Street from where we were working. And I recall those early days when I was getting involved in the Seigle Avenue church and its outreach and the formation of what would become Freedom School Partners, which would go on to run seventeen Freedom Schools in Charlotte and assist and inspire countless others throughout North Carolina and the country.

The Belmont neighborhood is north of uptown Charlotte just outside the I-277 loop. The neighborhood is part of a larger geography that includes the Villa Heights and Optimist Park communities. At the turn of the twentieth century, these three communities formed Charlotte's first entirely working-class suburban neighborhoods. Less than a fifteen-minute walk to Trade and Tryon Streets, the center of Charlotte, Belmont was also well served by the city's streetcar network at the time. The larger area contains three of the five surviving pre-1900s textile mill structures. The Alpha Mill, the Highland Park Mill #1, and the Louise Mill were the original economic engines of these neighborhoods and were served by the Seaboard rail line (CSX today). The Sugar Creek tributaries provided plenty of convenient water, a key ingredient in textile production and necessary for obtaining fire insurance at the time. In the areas between the textile mills, private developers built subdivisions for mill workers. The housing architecture was remarkably uniform with wooden variations of the Victorian and bungalow styles, both popular at the time.

In 1940, Piedmont Courts, North Carolina's oldest public housing community, was built in the heart of Belmont, originally to support low-income whites. As a product of the Jim Crow era, Belmont, like other suburban neighborhoods of Charlotte, had only white residents up through the early 1960s. By 1970, however, this had radically changed. Urban renewal efforts demolished thousands of homes in the nearby Brooklyn and Greenville neighborhoods in downtown Charlotte, displacing the black residents there. This created demand for housing in nearby Belmont, still close to public transportation and walkable to the mills.

Throughout the 1960s, Piedmont Courts transitioned to an all-black public housing community managed by the Charlotte Housing Authority. The "white flight" from the neighborhood was supported by Charlotte's sprawling suburban expansion, made possible by an extensive road system.

As the textile industry faded, the neighborhood declined due to a lack of reinvestment by the city, lenders, and residents. From 1970 to 1985, the population dropped by a third from 4,412 to 3,000. Over 40 percent of the housing stock was deteriorated or unoccupied. Unlike the higher-income suburbs, the Piedmont Courts infrastructure was largely ignored. In fact, the city began parking its smelly garbage trucks and putting noisy vehicle maintenance facilities in the large parcels where housing had been torn down. The dilapidated Piedmont Courts neighborhood became notorious for gangs, drugs, and crime, including numerous murders. The older citizens who might have helped to control the youth had been segregated into senior housing, located blocks away.

This historic community and its people have seen many changes, but lately most of them have been positive. Habitat for Humanity has played a tremendous role in the neighborhood, providing homes for more than a hundred families. Belmont today is evolving in racial and economic diversity. The desolate Piedmont Courts project has been replaced by Seigle Point, an attractive development of apartments and townhouses for hundreds of families, many of whom are making less than 30 percent of median income.

I'm proud of what my colleagues and I have been able to contribute, but still I feel pangs of regret. As one who has been in the thick of things here as the redeveloper of Piedmont Courts, I know this: we could have come a lot further were it not for politics and bureaucracy.

> **We could have come a lot further were it not for politics and bureaucracy.**

PUTTING FAITH INTO PRACTICE

By the turn of the millennium, the Piedmont Courts housing project was in desperate need of physical revival, and the streets had become an open drug market. I recall arriving for church on a Sunday morning and feeling the tension in the air: three people had been murdered in Piedmont Courts that morning. It was devastating news but not all that surprising. The congregation prayed for the violence to end.

And we didn't stop with prayers. For many years this congregation had been putting its faith into practice by advocating on behalf of the Piedmont Courts residents. Known as "the little church with a big mission," the church attracted progressive Christians with a desire to serve the community.

In fact, the church's focus since opening in 1945 was ministering to the residents of Piedmont Courts. Before the first service, congregants hand delivered a brochure to every door there declaring their desire "to share an inspired fellowship that breaks down racial and class barriers."

The public housing project, the city's first, was just four years old at the time. The Charlotte Housing Authority had torn down several dozen ramshackle wooden homes where textile mill workers had lived, making way for hundreds of brick apartment units. The rents were between $9.40 and $14 per month. To be eligible to move in, families had to have an income of no more than $724 to $1,166 a year, depending on the number of dependents. And they had to be white.

That changed after 1964 when the Civil Rights Act was supposed to lead to the integration of public housing. The housing authority immediately began desegregating its developments. Meanwhile, the idea of urban renewal had been to simply bulldoze historically black neighborhoods such as Greenville and Brooklyn, intensifying the demand for affordable housing. Many of those displaced families moved into the public housing at Piedmont Courts. And in an atmosphere of fear and distrust, most, if not all, of the white families moved out of Belmont, resulting in a failed desegregation attempt as the all-white community just became an all-black neighborhood.

During the white flight of the late 1960s and early '70s, local churches began following their former congregations into the suburbs. Seigle Avenue Presbyterian, however, was determined not to close its doors, though it felt the pressure. The congregation was still all-white, for now, but the pastor at the time, the Rev. Bill Stewart, chose to stay and desegregate the church. A few black children began trickling into the Sunday school and church programs.[13]

13   Information about the history of Seigle Avenue Presbyterian can be found in Margaret G. Bigger and Katherine M. Dunlap, *Small Church with a Big Mission: The History of the First 50 Years of the Seigle Avenue Presbyterian Church* (Charlotte, NC: A Borough Books, 1995).

Within a few months, 80 percent of the former white membership was gone, along with much of the church leadership who disagreed with such radical change. The Rev. Stewart heard stern warnings that black and white teenagers had been seen fraternizing and visiting one another's homes and who knew what else. The children had even been swimming together at day camp—was the pastor really going to allow such a thing?

Sitting on the sanctuary steps one evening, gazing over at the housing project across the avenue, a saddened Stewart pondered how much had been lost, but he saw how much could be gained. *Jesus loves the children over there*, he thought, *as much as those on this side of the street.* "At the foot of the cross," he later remarked, "the ground is level."

The leadership and determination of this man and a stalwart group of forward-thinking congregants turned Seigle Avenue Presbyterian into one of the city's first integrated churches. A few key members stayed and helped him reach out to the new black families moving into the neighborhood.

By the time I joined, the church had a congregation that appeared on any given Sunday to be around 40 percent African American and 60 percent Caucasian. It was a truly welcoming community where members felt comfortable no matter their sexual orientation or racial makeup. Smitty Flynn knew how to recruit the best singers—the House of Blues never sounded as good as the Sunday gospel his choir belted out.

I found that church to be not only a fun place, but one where you could see the daily impact of your contributions. The neighborhood truly needed it. Piedmont Courts remained a tough place to live, and the government had turned its back on the community.

FRUSTRATED HOPES

The Seigle Avenue Presbyterian Church was set up by a coalition of Presbyterian churches, and its charter said it was created to serve the people of Piedmont Courts, not just the white people of Piedmont Courts. Rev. Stewart held fast to his principles, and the church found ways to pursue that mission. They used the church facilities and resources to launch innovative programs, including high school completion classes, a hot meals program for the elderly, and well-baby clinics. In its service to Piedmont Courts, the church set up nonprofit groups to attract donations from outside the congregation. The first was the Seigle Avenue Preschool, a state-of-the-art facility for the children of Piedmont Courts. It set up a program called Jacob's Ladder, focusing on job training and career paths for the adults of the community. Those were in place before I became a member. Then, in 2000, the church funded Seigle Avenue Partners to run an after-school and summer program. Having been reluctant to get involved in church politics, I saw this as my best opportunity to contribute. I joined as the third board member of the new nonprofit.

About that time, the Charlotte Housing Authority saw an opportunity to get a federal Hope VI block grant to redevelop Piedmont Courts. I agreed to assist in representing the church and the neighborhood to work with the housing authority on what that redevelopment might entail. HUD initially denied a grant but eventually approved $20 million to turn the twenty-three acres into a mixed-income development of apartments, condos, and townhomes.

Meanwhile, the Joan B. Kroc Foundation donated $1.6 billion from the McDonald's fortune to the Salvation Army to open Kroc Centers in cities across the nation. The gift was the largest ever given to a charity at the time. The centers were conceived as forums for opportunity, education, recreation, and inspiration that could change neighborhoods and lives. Charles Woodyard, the CEO of Charlotte Housing Authority, and other local leaders approached me about the possibility that one could be established in Belmont. Would I be willing to champion the effort to secure a Kroc Center for the neighborhood?

It seemed like a once-in-a-lifetime opportunity. I agreed to take up the cause, so long as all parties would collaborate without conflict. The community needed to show that it could produce sufficient support money through local fundraising as a matching gift. We worked on building consensus in the neighborhood and the surrounding area. I then spent about $50,000 of my own money trying to secure a grant—and we succeeded. The letter arrived with the good news: we would be getting a $75 million grant for a Kroc Center in Belmont.

Despite that incredible financial feat—and this was 2008, when Charlotte was about to face some of its bleakest economic times—those high hopes soon faded. The proposal became a political lightning rod. YMCA officials claimed that the Kroc Center would put one of their facilities out of business, a stance that made no sense considering how badly the neighborhood needed a wide array of services. I ended up in a shouting match with the chairman of the YMCA board of trustees. A city council member also opposed the plan for the center, even though the proposal was to establish it in the member's district. I was appalled. How could someone believe that helping this neighborhood wasn't a good idea?

As things got ugly, the Salvation Army decided to hire Ruth Samuelson as an intermediary and try to restart the process. As a North Carolina state representative, she would go on to champion many environmental movements. Despite her help, the process dragged on, and the Kroc Foundation eventually said enough was enough and pulled the grant. The Belmont neighborhood, and for that matter Charlotte, lost a major catalyst for change. In the depth of the 2008–09 recession, when that funding would have made a major impact on any community, Charlotte had blown its awarded $75 million grant. A Kroc Center would have been the perfect anchor to facilitate change. Instead, Charlotte's loss was a big gain for the people of Greenville, South Carolina. They now have an impressive Kroc Center on the edge of their downtown.

Instead of getting a beautiful Kroc Center as an anchor for opportunity near the new Seigle Apartments, the Belmont neighborhood continued to be the city's parking lot for its smelly garbage trucks. It was another example of politics hurting low-income areas. What city parks garbage trucks in a neighborhood?

United States Congressman Mel Watt, prior to becoming director of the Federal Housing Finance Agency, publicly called for the city to relocate the dump trucks when speaking at the Seigle Point groundbreaking. The airport director argued publicly for the facility to be moved to the airport. He said, "Garbage trucks don't complain about airplane noise." Instead, certain politicians felt that the trucks should stay in the Belmont neighborhood, where they still park as I write this.

At least the $20 million grant from HUD to redevelop Piedmont Courts was secured; however, the Charlotte Housing Authority decided to fire the developer that it originally chose. Once again, officials from the housing authority came to my office: would I be willing to take over? It was an awkward situation. My commitment to Belmont had been in a volunteer capacity; I hadn't planned to benefit commercially. I reached out to church members and others in the neighborhood on whom I had relied during early negotiations, and to my surprise they were thrilled that we would become the developer. Grubb Properties teamed with TCG Development Services, a group from Washington, DC, with experience in dealing with HUD and affordable housing. We matched the Hope VI grant with low-income housing tax credits and secured housing trust fund money from the city. We completed the first phase of Seigle Point ahead of schedule and well within the budget. In fact, the redevelopment came in $1 million under budget.

By this time, I had agreed to become the third chairman of the board for Seigle Avenue Partners. We had started operating our programs as Freedom Schools, a program set up and run by the Children's Defense Fund in Washington, DC. We had also started operating Freedom Schools in other neighborhoods. With the blessing of Marian Wright Edelman, the civil rights hero and founder of the Children's Defense Fund, we changed our name from Seigle Avenue Partners to Freedom School Partners. I arranged to put the organization's headquarters in the Seigle Point clubhouse along with its after-school and summer programs. I believe it is the only lease I have ever signed as both the landlord and the tenant. I guess sometimes conflicts can be a good thing.

I also worked out a deal that resulted in a public park with ten tennis courts, a soccer field, playgrounds, and half-court basketball. My son's private school, Trinity Episcopal School, was about two blocks away, and it was a young urban school with limited ball fields. Under the arrangement, the housing authority would lease the land for the project for a dollar a year for ninety-nine years; the school would raise enough money to build the facilities and infrastructure; and the parks and recreation department would maintain it as a public park. The collaboration came together beautifully. Trinity now has tennis and soccer facilities for practice and tournaments, and the community has a wonderful and active public park.

In addition to the exciting nonprofit and park initiatives, I was proud of the fact that my development team delivered the apartments ahead of schedule and under budget. Unfortunately, the fact that we came in $1 million under budget for Seigle Point didn't exactly please the Charlotte Housing Authority. In a rational world, you would think everyone would be impressed that we were able to leave that much money in the project's escrow account. The housing authority maintained, however, that under HUD regulations, it would get downgraded and lose federal funding unless it spent 100 percent of the money. The current administration of the housing authority had never experienced a developer coming in under budget, so it threatened a lawsuit against us for putting it in such a position. Talk about a backward process.

To straighten out that mess, we had to figure out how to spend another $1 million. We ended up adding some bridges and other unnecessary features just to appease the government bureaucracy, lest it cut off the housing authority's federal funding. It was a ridiculous scenario—but it just goes to show the problems with government-created bureaucracies. It sends the message that if you find ways to save the government some money, you will get punished.

Meanwhile, another part of the redevelopment proposal included townhomes that Grubb Properties was going to sell at market rate. A goal of the Hope VI plan was to stabilize the neighborhood to reduce crime and poverty. The way to do that is to attract a percentage of residents of better means who do not need subsidized housing. We were able to find buyers and presell every home prior to commencement of construction. In fact, on the first day they were on the market, we got signed contracts on twenty-four of the fifty townhomes that we planned to build and quickly signed contracts for the remaining homes over the next couple of weeks.[14] We eventually ended up with a long waiting list of prospects should any of the fifty signed contracts fall by the wayside.

As we were preparing to begin construction, our lender, Bank of America, pointed out that HUD still had a lien on the property. No problem, though, the bank said. All we needed was a simple, one-page release from HUD confirming that it was waiving any claim on the parcel per the approved plan filed on record. Once we obtained that, we could proceed.

The release confirming the already-approved plan took eleven months for HUD to write. The long delay prevented us from moving forward with the construction. Under condominium laws, one can't presell a home two years in advance. Given that it takes about a year to build the townhouses and we had now burned up an entire year waiting on HUD, we felt it prudent to go back to every buyer and ask them to sign a new contract. In effect saying, "Sorry, it's going to take a year longer than we expected before you can move in, are you still interested?" But the world had changed since we first asked HUD to write that letter, and the Great Recession was upon us. At this point, few folks were still interested in purchasing the townhomes, and every contract was virtually void.

After having been defeated in my pursuit for a Kroc Center and in my attempts to relocate the smelly garbage trucks, I was determined not to allow the new affordable housing at Seigle Point to become tomorrow's Piedmont Courts, an isolated and concentrated housing project. So I went to the Charlotte Housing Authority and pitched a creative solution to allow us to commence construction of thirty-one of the homes. The housing authority, appreciating what

14   "Townhomes at Former Piedmont Courts Site Popular with Buyers," HipHoods, April 3, 2007, http://www.hiphoods.com/blog/2007/04/03/townhomes-at-former-piedmont-courts-site-popular-with-buyers/.

we were trying to achieve, agreed to reduce the price of the land from over $1 million to just $4,000 per townhome, payable upon the closing of the sale of each home. It also secured $60,000 in subsidies for twenty of the future homeowners who would qualify under low-income programs. We felt that we still could sell the townhomes, especially with the first-time home buyer credit that was coming into play, but we didn't anticipate making any money on them. I felt, though, that profit wasn't the priority. What mattered most was to bring stability to the neighborhood and get the project finished. The whole process was extremely challenging, and we did end up losing money, but we were able to sell the thirty-one townhouses and continue improving the community. Sadly, a decade later we have still not built the remaining nineteen townhouses despite the need for such housing because of a number of lingering issues and economic challenges, which we have hopefully finally resolved.

My experience in Belmont is one of great hope given all that we have accomplished but it is also one of great frustration. During this multidecade process, I was exposed to significant inefficiencies, disincentives, and friction on how we tackle community building. I was truly amazed by the negative impact that government bureaucracy and decades of poor federal and local public policy can have on a community. I was also surprised by how difficult it would be to create and sustain momentum even after pouring so many resources into the effort.

Fortunately, the Belmont revival has gained traction despite the neighborhood's inherent challenges. Primarily, a lot of credit goes to the fact that Charlotte has been blessed with a strong economy, and the pressure to expand the center city has helped nearby Belmont. After a decade of stagnation, the area is seeing an influx of more townhomes and mixed-income housing. As the momentum builds, it looks as if the neighborhood will get over the hump.

WHY WE NEED TO KEEP REINVENTING

In 1961, Jane Jacobs in her groundbreaking book, *The Life and Death of Great American Cities,* warned us of entrenched bureaucracies and the damage they can do to our cities. Unfortunately, HUD, despite the good intentions of so many of the folks who work there, has become such an entity. The agency distributing the tax money that is needed to solve our housing crisis is also an agency that can be maddeningly frustrating. The weight of its bureaucracy makes it averse to trying new things, even when those innovations would save money and provide more affordable housing.

How does it make sense, for example, to reject a much-needed housing development that could bring reasonable rents to a neighborhood just because HUD cannot understand the benefit of sharing commercial and residential parking to reduce development costs? I say this because I recently had a loan rejected for that specific reason. And why must it take a year and a half or longer for HUD to approve a construction loan, when any lender in the open market can approve a similar one in a matter of weeks? The only reason developers tolerate such a long delay for securing a development loan under HUD's 221(d)4 program is the attractive interest rate and forty-two-year fixed-rate financing. These useful but hard-to-access tools are used to perpetuate the bureaucracy. HUD points to its 221(d)4 program as a source of profit to allow it to further facilitate its mission, but I'm not sure who is doing the accounting. If a private-sector lender took close to ten times longer than a typical competitor to process a loan, it would be insolvent pretty quickly.

Many landlords simply cannot afford to deal with HUD's bureaucratic system. Section 8 vouchers, which are issued to very low-income families, the elderly, and the disabled, are a prime example. We would love to be able to accept these vouchers in some of the five thousand apartments we operate. In fact, we have some of our apartments set aside for families making below 30 percent of median income, but we don't accept Section 8 vouchers. HUD's restrictive policies scare us off and tend to push most of the best landlords away. A landlord who takes a Section 8 voucher from one resident will be required to open every single unit in the apartment community to the vouchers. The landlords are also forced to go through extensive inspections that often feel arbitrary and punitive. The headaches don't make economic sense. The *New York Times* recently did a study in Philadelphia that determined the majority of landlords refuse such vouchers.[15]

Participating in programs like Section 8 involves too many rules and regulations for most landlords, many of whom struggle enough without the extra burdens the government bureaucracy brings. Meanwhile, the legal services and other nonprofits that are strong advocates for renters sometimes add additional costs to landlords as well. I know a specific example of a renter who damaged a home, kicked out the screens, and declared, "I don't have to pay my rent! I've got a bad landlord!" Legal Aid often comes to their rescue, as do other advocates. Examples where the system rallies around a tenant who clearly has damaged property hurt everyone.

> I believe we can create policies where the agencies and landlords work together to create win/win scenarios that allow lower-income families greater access to a variety of housing options.

---

15   Glenn Thrush, "With Market Hot, Landlords Slam the Door on Section 8 Tenants," *New York Times*, October 12, 2018.

Sure, there are bad landlords who have abused the system, but the great majority are doing their best to do the right thing and don't wish to be presumed guilty until proved innocent. The attitude creates an us versus them mentality that is toxic. I believe we can create policies where the agencies and landlords work together to create win/win scenarios that allow lower-income families greater access to a variety of housing options.

These are talented professionals who could do a lot toward solving the affordable housing crisis—but where's the incentive to get involved? Richard Florida, in doing his research, determined that middle classes are larger and tend to be stronger in more conservative communities than the more liberal/progressive communities, which I found quite odd. However, this may just go to show that sometimes probusiness policies are actually the more progressive policies.

Just as Jane Jacobs warned us about government bureaucracies, HUD seems more focused on protecting its own fate than on promoting affordable housing. I am told that its union contract for HUD employees stretches four hundred pages, right down to the kinds of snacks that can go into the vending machines. A lot of those people are competent and interested in the mission of improving urban housing, but dealing with bureaucracies tends to eventually drive the most talented individuals away to other pursuits—if they don't turn into zombies. Personally, I think it has gotten to the point where HUD's inefficiencies are incapable of being corrected. I am confident we could spend the department's $53 billion budget more impactfully.

In reality, federal policies are doing little to promote affordable housing at a time of crisis. Despite the great investment opportunity for the private sector, some of the best developers stay away from affordable housing because they don't want to deal with HUD or other arbitrary measures beyond their control. I am confident that if those developers instead knew that they could start on a level playing field with a predictable path to completion, they would be more willing to participate in finding solutions. As it stands, affordable housing has become more expensive to build than market-rate housing. The largest multifamily contractor in Charlotte, John Huson, sums it up best: "The most affordable housing I build is market-rate housing; the least affordable housing I build is what they call affordable housing." He claims that because of government regulations, it costs 20 to 30 percent more to build a unit of affordable housing than a comparable market-rate apartment home. Such is the frustration of dealing with all the governmental red tape.

We need a fresh way of thinking that in no way holds on to the concept of packing poor people together into housing projects, out of sight and out of mind. It never worked. It fostered crime and perpetuated segregation. Segregation is one of the greatest obstacles to economic mobility. Our nation needs diverse communities where poor people live near their more affluent neighbors for the betterment of all.

CREATIVE APPROACHES

If we could unlock all the brain power and entrepreneurial resources of the private sector toward the mission, the supply of affordable housing would increase dramatically. Our society needs creative approaches that will get financing for homeownership into the hands of those who need it most and do so efficiently. It hasn't been happening that way. The lending abuses of the early 2000s were serious, but the overreaction led to stifling overregulation that is proving just as devastating to the people who are simply trying to get ahead. Not long ago, you could get a home loan if you could breathe when prices were sky high. This encouraged our most vulnerable people to purchase homes at unsustainable prices and create rampant speculation. Following the great financial crisis, when housing prices were cheapest and we could do the most to help improve people's living status, even the most deserving and qualified applicants could not get a home loan.

Consider this: Ben Bernanke bought a Washington townhouse in 2004 for $839,000, a few years before he became chairman of the Federal Reserve. In 2014, after finishing his second term there, he applied for a loan to refinance his $672,000 mortgage. He was turned down. It wasn't because the house wouldn't have appraised sufficiently—its value had been stable. It wasn't his income level—he was still making big bucks as a Brookings Institute economist as well as getting $250,000 per speech. The problem? He had recently changed jobs. He couldn't show two years of stable income from the same source, a rule originating with the government bureaucracy. Any lender with basic discretion would have looked at Bernanke's million-dollar's-plus assets and approved the loan, but in the over-regulated, shell-shocked world of mortgage finance, he was deemed unfit for a home loan.[16]

In another example, Deidre lent a friend the money to buy a condo. They had figured they could get the friend a home loan, and Deidre even offered to cosign, but after close to two years of trying it was still a no-go. In this example, you had a single mother with enough assets to pay for her home in cash, you had a guarantor with significantly more liquid assets and income to support the mortgage, and it was a fruitless and frustrating experience. They killed several trees submitting paperwork, with nothing to show for it.

16   Neil Irwin, "Why Ben Bernanke Can't Refinance His Mortgage," *New York Times*, Oct. 2, 2014, https://www.nytimes.com/2014/10/03/upshot/why-ben-bernanke-cant-refinance-his-mortgage.html.

Grubb Properties also felt the frustration at Seigle Point in the Belmont neighborhood, where we built those thirty-one townhouses at market rate on the site of the old Piedmont Courts. For every application that we managed to get approved for a loan to buy a townhome, forty-nine others were rejected. Getting a simple primary home loan became an impossible task at a time when homes were the absolute cheapest they had been in years. It would have been a perfect time to advance economic mobility for so many, but the over-reaction with overregulation got in the way of the best intentions.

Since I am venting my frustration with government policies, it is worth including the student loan debacle and the impact it is having on future generations' ability to secure housing and on the destruction of economic mobility. I believe education is critical to the advancement of people and our democratic society, so please don't take the following comments as a criticism of education itself. According to the May 13, 2019, article by Howard Gold in the *Chicago Booth Review*, "for-profit colleges enroll 10 percent of US students but account for 50 percent of student loan defaults. And low-income students are hit the hardest."[17] Examples of these colleges include Trump University, which had to pay a $25 million fine. While we were cracking down on these colleges, "Secretary DeVos rescinded the 'gainful employment' rule and loosened accreditation standards, giving some former operators with poor track records a second chance." Unfortunately, many students don't even get their diplomas. Can you imagine racking up over $50,000 in debt for a degree you did not receive or an education you never got? I recently heard a television ad that offered a free laptop for signing up for a for-profit college.

---

17   Howard Gold, "Who's At Fault for Student-Loan Defaults?" Chicago Booth Review, May 13, 2019, https://review.chicagobooth.edu/public-policy/2019/article/who-s-fault-student-loan-defaults.

The fact that the government has not gotten out of this business is embarrassing and expensive. The result has been rampant educational inflation, making the cost less affordable to the masses. Student loans used to be made by the private sector with the government guaranteeing 98 percent, so lenders had at least a little skin in the game. I think the colleges should be held accountable. If a school's students cannot repay their loans, then future students at that particular school should not qualify for loans. That would weed out the colleges that aren't serious about education and would incentivize them to also educate their students on the importance of their credit and paying off their obligations, a valuable lesson that would benefit all of society.

Government policies should inspire and regulate, but the government should not try to compete. It never will be as efficient and innovative as the private sector.

I have nothing against for-profit colleges. Some do a great job of educating their students—just as some nonprofit colleges do a poor job. What I oppose are policies that the government thinks it can execute better than the private sector. We need a system that rewards progress and penalizes abuse. Capitalism is a great system because it inspires innovation. Government policies should inspire and regulate, but the government should not try to compete. It never will be as efficient and innovative as the private sector. It should not be implementing student loans—nor should it be building and owning housing.

INNOVATION IS THE ANSWER

It wasn't the people getting loans of $150,000 or less for their primary homes that created the great financial crisis. They're not the culprits, but they are the ones being punished. Government policies should help hardworking families who want to buy affordable homes. Fannie Mae and Freddie Mac have played a huge role in stabilizing the multifamily business and allowing it to continue to attract capital dollars, even during the recession. Without that, our supply-and-demand imbalance would be significantly worse. So I am not proposing that government doesn't have a role. But government should be a facilitator, not an implementer.

The most important role government can play is in providing a safety net not only to our most fragile citizens but to the majority of them. Life happens, and at some point we all need support. Some have wonderful family networks, but others don't. There is a better way.

STARTER HOME FINANCING: A BETTER WAY

Getting a starter home should be much easier. We shouldn't have the same rules for the buyer of a $100,000 home as we have for the buyer of a $500,000 home. A 20 percent deposit makes sense for the more expensive home, but buyers of affordable starter homes who have good credit shouldn't have to provide the same type of deposit.

Government policymakers should consider the price of the primary home when figuring the percentage of deposit that is required to buy it. They should pay more attention to how that price relates to median prices in its neighborhood.

For example, I would be in favor of the following: If the house is less than half the median price in the neighborhood, the buyers should be able to secure 100 percent financing. If the price is approximately at the median price, the buyer gets 90 percent financing. It would be 80 percent for homes selling between median price to no more than 150 percent of the median. If buyers want a home that costs more than 150 percent of the median price, let them secure their loan on the private market with no government participation.

JP-Morgan Chase just put out a new study about the impacts on loan modifications in the crisis, and one of the most interesting aspects from it was that loan to value and principal reduction modifications had almost zero impact on default ratios. It was income to payment amount (and the existence of a safety net of some kind for when trouble occurred) that mattered most. Three months of payments in a savings account was one of the best indicators for success. Therefore, the few precious resources that families have trying to get ahead should not be tied up in a down payment but put into a savings program, along with an emergency line of credit, to help assist for when life happens.

I think having a policy that is more focused on home values which helps prop up struggling neighborhoods and avoids subsidizing rich neighborhoods is the right approach for our government agencies. The idea is a plan that subsidizes more affordable homes in a neighborhood and provides no support for the new McMansions that often appear as gentrification takes over a neighborhood. That way the agencies have more loans and less concentration, and they are getting people who would benefit the most from homeownership into houses and helping to fulfill their American Dream. We are creating greater equity for our most fragile, which in the long run reduces the cost to society and makes us a stronger and safer nation.

Housing policy need not be complicated. To stimulate the construction of affordable housing, the government must make the effort worthwhile for the private sector. That's where change will happen. The proper role for government is to provide incentives for industries to flourish, not to hamstring them. The new opportunity zone tax incentives are going to play an interesting role in this evolution, and I look forward to seeing how it plays out. However, we do need regulations, of course. The government should protect families from predatory lending and other abuses, and the penalties should be severe. The government's functions are essential but must not go too far—and it goes too far when it stymies the ability of private enterprise to solve our society's many challenges. The government's job is to encourage the best minds to focus on the pressing issues before us. Its role is to provide oversight to ensure that everyone is playing fair—but it shouldn't be playing the game itself.

What is lacking is a vision and commitment to finding a solution. That won't come from holding tight to the status quo and protecting turf. Together we can design a better system, but time is of the essence. We must get started now in defining what that would look like. I'm not saying I have all the answers. I'm saying that we cannot afford to put off looking for all the answers. To solve the current crisis, the government needs to dramatically shrink its role and focus its energy on encouraging private enterprise to meet the demand in innovative ways.

The housing crisis we have in front of us will be perhaps the largest in the modern history of our country. It will take new thinking. It will require a willingness to abandon what no longer works, or never did. It will take passion and commitment. Our communities require this of us, and the future of our country depends on it.

Our collective focus must be on lifting people up, on motivating them rather than warehousing them. I admire the Habitat for Humanity slogan: "A hand up, not a handout." That's the spirit that drives those volunteers to wake up and hammer away in the morning sunshine, day after day, to build something better in communities across the country. The program pushes people to be their best and rewards them for their efforts. That's how Deidre and I felt as we joined a work team in Belmont, years ago, when Cherlonda was small and we had so very far to go. And that's the attitude that will take us the rest of the way.

CHAPTER 6

THE TALK OF
THE TOWN

> *Many people still see urbanization as a destructive force—but urban living can lead to more efficient use of resources and smaller carbon footprints.*

Pascal Mittermaier, The Nature Conservancy

SMALL-TOWN LIVING WAS ATTRACTIVE when I was young. Jobs were plentiful and paid well, and the amenities were wonderful. In the 1960s and 1970s, Lexington, where I grew up, was a fully functioning micro-economy, like many cities in North Carolina and elsewhere in the South. People who lived in the town generally worked, shopped, learned, played, and prayed there.

By the late 1980s and 1990s, however, metropolitan growth—fueled by the interstates, regional retail business, and suburban housing development—had rapidly changed these cities, particularly the historic downtowns. Instead of shopping locally, people could easily drive for miles to malls and shopping centers. Skilled workers could now get better pay by commuting to the new suburban office parks of Greensboro or Charlotte. Regional coliseums and other attractions changed patterns of civic events and recreation.

The downtowns suffered. Stores closed, small businesses relocated, and investment dried up. Communities were losing what little economic diversification they had—such as the furniture and textile industries on which my hometown long had depended.

Growing up in Lexington, I knew a lot of kids whose dream was to get a job at the furniture factory, where they figured they would be set for life. At one point, Dixie Furniture Company alone employed over thirty-two hundred people, which was approximately 20 percent of the entire population of Lexington. Dixie Furniture had long been a stalwart of the community. To work there was the height of ambition for many a sixteen-year-old all too eager to get on with life—so why wait to get a diploma? If the company hired you, you had it made. I had classmates whose families had worked there for generations. The company had grown from a small manufacturing shop that opened in 1901 to eventually cover thirty-one acres and nine downtown blocks near the tracks of the Southern Railway.

Dixie Furniture thrived for decades, along with the local textile industry, but in time the competition from imports hit both industries hard. In 1987, new management renamed the company Lexington Furniture Industries, and after a buyout in 1996, it became Lexington Home Brands. The new owners sold it to senior managers in 2002. Eventually, the word came down to the workers on the factory floor: the plants were closing. The company's chief executive officer explained that the buildings were outdated and couldn't support low-cost manufacturing techniques. And by then, about half the company's new products were imports.

Thousands of workers lost their jobs. My brothers and I put

our heads together to figure out what we might do to help our hometown. We decided that our best approach would be to donate enough money to establish a small community college branch, just around two thousand square feet, in downtown Lexington, where those laid-off employees would have access to get the training they needed to pursue another occupation.

A couple of years later, I stopped in to see how well our investment was helping the community, and a college representative took me on a tour of the facilities. "How many people have been coming in for classes?" I asked her.

"You wouldn't believe it!" she said. "In the past two years we've been open, over four thousand people have come through." I was amazed and felt a real sense of pride and accomplishment. Talk about a return on investment! All those folks getting an education and a new lease on life.

"So what kind of subjects were they studying?" I asked, imagining an assortment of tech and trade offerings.

She looked at me, a little puzzled. "Every one of them was working on a GED," she said. "None of them had high school diplomas."

My heart sank, and I felt a wave of nausea. These were people I grew up with, but I had no idea that so many had dropped out of high school. They had charted a future in their little town working on the assembly line, and now the plant was closed. They lacked a lot of the basic skills needed in today's economy. *The chances of attracting a modern industry to this town are going to be impossible*, I thought. *Those companies will be looking for a more qualified workforce.*

In real estate, location is king, and without a promising future for Lexington, real estate values plummeted. When I joined the company full time in 1993, my brothers and I recognized the demographic changes occurring. I set a goal that year of liquidating everything we owned in Davidson County, which unfortunately I had not fully achieved when the global financial crisis of 2008 occurred. A prime example was a twenty-acre tract on the main retail street in town. It was an entire block that my brothers and I owned with another family directly across from the cinema, with Winn-Dixie on one side and Kmart on the other. In 1993, we sold an acre and a half for $150,000, so we knew the whole tract was worth at least $100,000 an acre—and no doubt a whole lot more considering that what we sold was a back parcel without any street frontage. We still owned both corners of the block and all the frontage. The remaining eighteen and a half acres were easily worth a couple million dollars at the time.

Over twenty years later, in 2016, our partner who owned a percentage of the land notified me that he wanted out and suggested that we work out a buy/sell agreement. I told him I was comfortable with an arrangement where he would set a number on the entire parcel and I would decide whether we would be the buyer or the seller. He felt that was fair and said he would think about it. A week later he called back with his assessment of the value—$150,000, and that wasn't per acre. He was putting a price of $150,000 on the entire eighteen and a half acres, a block of retail frontage on what is still one of the more vibrant streets in town, though that vibrancy was dying quickly. That's how much we had gotten for just that small parcel we sold nearly a quarter century earlier.

"Let me talk to my brothers, and I'll get back to you," I said. After little debate, we all agreed that we were sellers despite the low price applied to the property. I called him back. "We think you've got a fair number. We're a seller." After a long pause, I heard a stutter: "Uh, but I'm not sure I'm a buyer." It was quite shocking to see a parcel unable to sell in 2016 for less than 10 percent of its 1993 value. Our partner eventually bought my brothers and me out of the land at that price, but it was about a year and a half later.

Another example illustrating the devastating impact that these small towns suffered upon losing their factories was a development that my family had next to the country club in Lexington. My father's uncle had donated the golf course for the country club with a deed restriction that the golf course would remain public. It is probably the only country club where you must be a member to eat in the restaurant or swim in the pool but where anyone can play on the golf course. My mother's family had a large farm adjacent to the country club, and my father showed them how to develop it. In the 1970s, it became the premier neighborhood in Lexington. We could easily sell a half acre to an acre lot for $60,000, and the proceeds provided a nice lifestyle for my grandparents and their children and grand-children. Fast forward to 2015, when our extended family of nine cousins still owned seventy-five acres of that land. It had been years since we had sold a single lot. The last transaction had been a half acre sold to the adjacent homeowner for $12,000.

One of my cousins came up with the bright idea of clear-cut-ting the timber on those seventy-five acres. All I could imagine was how irate the neighbors would be if their country club area now had seventy-five acres of clear-cut land. I had visions of Dr. Seuss's Lorax, who "speaks for the trees," scolding me for chopping them down. After talking it through with my brothers and aunt, however, we decided that doing so was in the best fiduciary interest of the extended family—but we agreed to give the neighborhood plenty of notice and make sure to replant all the trees.

The venom spewed as neighbors lied about promises my parents had made to them and tried to guilt us out of moving forward with our plans. As a compromise, the family agreed to sell the remaining acreage to the neighbors at the bargain basement price of just $4,000 an acre. That was just $300,000 for our remaining seventy-five acres, right behind a house known as the castle. I am confident both that the owner spent over $4 million to build that castle house and that it was the largest home in Lexington. We gave the neighbors six months to come up with the money, but they couldn't do it. Sadly, the sale didn't go through, even at that price and in the heart of the country club neighborhood. As a result, we clear-cut the land and replanted it, netting the family over $75,000 and retaining 100 percent of its ownership. The castle eventually was sold at auction for under $700,000, less than 20 percent of what it cost to build. The castle has since been donated to a nonprofit, and it is supposedly used for church services today.

The story of what happened in Lexington is not unique. It was once a thriving community where many of the children went to work in the factories, though some went on to Harvard, Duke, and other great colleges. Today, few of its high school graduates leave North Carolina. Sadly, this story has played out thousands of times in mill towns all over the United States, leaving communities desperate to participate in today's thriving economy. While we can't reverse the devastation of yesterday, we can chart a clear path for a brighter future.

The lesson is clear enough. Municipalities need to invest in their workforce by developing local talent.

DEVELOPING THE TALENT

The lesson is clear enough. Municipalities need to invest in their workforce by developing local talent. They also need to figure out ways to attract skilled millennials to move to town. We are seeing the resurgence of these small downtowns led by people such as Vivian Howard, a celebrity chef who moved back to her hometown of Kinston, North Carolina, and is leading a culinary resurgence there with local breweries and competitive restaurant and entertainment options. That's the kind of entrepreneurial spirit that is required today to attract industries and businesses to bring greater vibrancy to a community.

To avoid being vulnerable, municipalities must invest in the future. It starts with education. Unfortunately, today's educational opportunities seem to ignore the many trade opportunities that exist and are in high demand. Many young people are only exposed to specific jobs, primarily in service industries. For example, the construction industry is facing a massive shortage of tradespeople, and the current workers are getting older. Plumbers and electricians these days are typically in their late fifties, and a lot of them will be retiring soon even though the demand for their services has been increasing significantly, according to the Bureau of Labor Statistics.[18] Yet young people haven't seemed interested in taking up the trades. I don't know if that is because their parents and guidance counselors haven't encouraged them to do so, schools have shifted away from those courses, or those jobs are just too demanding.

I saw a troubling statistic recently related to construction labor. A significant number of those jobs were lost during the financial crisis of 2008–09, but despite the continued growth since, the labor pool for construction continues to decline. As a result, it's hard to find enough folks to fill the positions of those retiring, let alone to keep up with the ever-growing demand for new homes and apartments.

The result has been dramatic inflation as we witness the cost to

18   See the Bureau's "Occupational Outlook Handbook" for construction and extraction occupations at https://www.bls.gov/ooh/construction-and-extraction.

build a new home or apartment exceeding what most families can afford. Today the average new home cost is approaching $400,000. The only way to bring down the cost is by increasing construction efficiency.

The labor shortage remains the greatest impediment to affordable housing throughout the United States—and as cities seek to solve that problem and develop their workforces, those people will need places to live. Virtually every growing city in America is struggling to house its workforce. Even though the bulk of the new construction has been in these urban areas, it is still not at a pace that can keep up with demand.

We in America need to radically transform our approach to housing. I recently visited Singapore, probably the most successful country in improving its GDP over the past fifty years, and was impressed to learn that basic housing for everyone was a key component of its success. In Singapore, the government provides housing at a subsidized rate. Residents buy their homes and get the benefits and burdens of market fluctuations. They have the pride of ownership and a stake in improving their community. The concept of subsidized housing that is owned by the resident is incomprehensible in most of America, but it is the primary principle on which Grubb Properties originally was built. With today's low interest rates, what better time to create a nationwide homeownership subsidy program? As mentioned in chapter five, JP-Morgan Chase's study showed that equity in a home had little bearing on defaults; it was cash flow and the availability of some type of safety net when life happened.

A TALE OF THREE CITIES

In researching what many US cities have been doing to address the issue, I have been unable to find a good example of one that has done so adequately. Three cities I have reviewed—Seattle, Nashville, and Denver—have done better than most in responding to the need to develop affordable housing, but the results still have been woefully inadequate.

Seattle

Seattle, Washington, had the not-so-proud distinction in 2017 of making the top-five list of the most expensive cities for renters in the United States, according to a census report based on figures from the previous year. The median rent that was being paid for all apartments in the city had gone up nearly $100 in the annual survey to $1,448. (The highest that year was San Jose, California, at $1,919; the lowest was Wichita, Kansas, at $762.)[19]

Seattle city officials knew that they had to do something, or the high costs would keep away or force out a lot of smart folks. Seattle was at risk of a brain drain that could sap its vitality. Despite the soaring rents, the rental demand was rising—since the start of the decade, Seattle had seen an increase of nearly 20 percent in the number of people living in apartments.

A few years earlier, in 2014, when Seattle made the top-ten list of most expensive cities for renters, city officials began brainstorming ways to make housing more available and affordable and came up with eight key strategies:

→ Require that new housing developments include affordable units and that commercial developments pay a fee to support affordable housing.

19 Gene Balk, "Seattle Rents Now Rank among Top 5 Most Expensive in US; Tacoma Joins $1,000 Club," *Seattle Times*, December 6, 2017, https://www.seattletimes.com/seattle-news/data/seattle-rents-now-rank-among-top-5-most-expensive-in-u-s-tacoma-joins-1000-rent-club/; Gregory Scruggs, "Homeless in Seattle Celebrate $3 Billion Affordable Housing Victory," *Reuters*, March 29, 2018, https://www.reuters.com/article/us-usa-housing-funding/homeless-in-seattle-celebrate-3-billion-affordable-housing-victory-idUSKBN1H51RV.

→ Devote more land to multifamily housing, particularly near transit, services, and amenities. Allow taller buildings and adjust codes to permit less expensive wood-frame construction.

→ Preserve the existing multifamily housing by acquiring properties, offer a property tax exemption to private landlords who agree to restrict rent, and fund subsidies for extremely low-income households.

→ Secure more resources with a real estate excise tax to fund affordable housing and an expansion of the State Housing Trust Fund. Use more public property for affordable housing and dedicate property taxes from new construction to affordable housing.

→ Renew the Seattle Housing Levy, a property tax to fund affordable housing and support vulnerable families.

→ Provide funding for tenant counseling and landlord education to prevent displacement and increase access.

→ Encourage people to set up apartments in their houses or outbuildings by removing code barriers. Allow more housing variety in single-family zones, such as cottages, duplexes, and triplexes.

→ Help to cut construction costs by completing design and historic reviews more efficiently and reducing the number of projects that must undergo environmental review.

Seattle has made progress in instituting some of those recommendations. For one, voters in 2016 renewed the housing levy. "Too many longtime residents are getting locked out and pushed out of

Seattle," Mayor Jenny Durkan explained. The $290 million levy was twice the amount approved seven years prior. The next year, the city announced that it would double its annual spending on affordable housing projects to $100 million, including investments in nine new apartment buildings and twenty-six homes for first-time buyers.

The city also has been reviewing its zoning laws to support the new Mandatory Housing Affordability Program. Under the policy, developers of new housing projects will have to include affordable homes, and commercial developers will have to contribute to a city fund for affordable housing.

To help reduce the costs of that construction, the city council in 2018 expanded where developers can build housing without including off-street parking. The exemption had been allowed only in areas with "frequent transit service"—and so the city broadened its definition of what that constituted. Meanwhile, the city adopted new rules to let landlords rent out parking spaces to people who don't live or work in their buildings, and tenants now can opt out of parking to get a lower rent. The aim of the legislation is to encourage mass transit and bicycling and to better match the supply of parking with the demand for it.

To encourage homeowners to set up apartments in their houses or in backyard structures, Seattle also reconsidered its restrictions on those "accessory dwelling units." Those restrictions dictated how many units were allowed, their size and location, who could occupy them, and parking requirements. Under the new rules, a homeowner could offer both in-house and detached apartments, even on a smaller lot. The house no longer would have to be owner-occupied for six months. The units could be larger, and no off-street parking would be required.

Nashville

In a May 2017 housing report, Nashville's mayor pointed out that the city's growth had created exciting possibilities but was also making it hard for many residents to stay.[20] For half the renters and one-quarter of the homeowners, the cost of housing had risen to more than 30 percent of their income, a level considered to be "cost-burdened." That hurts the economy because residents have less money to spend elsewhere.

The report noted that companies looking to move into Nashville often asked whether the city had enough housing for its workers. It said the demand for housing was strong, pushing up rental prices. The city was addressing the problem, the report said, with nearly nineteen hundred affordable and "workforce" units preserved, planned, or under construction, but the mayor conceded there was still much to do.

Nashville has committed tens of millions of dollars to the Barnes Housing Trust Fund since city officials set it up in 2013. It is funded by short-term rental permits and provides grants to nonprofit housing developers to increase affordable options. The city also initiated two ordinances offering incentives such as tax abatement and zoning concessions to motivate for-profit builders to include more afford-able units in their developments, but neither program was attracting much interest.

The city council in 2017 also approved a $25 million bond issue so that the city could buy existing low-income housing at risk of being acquired by developers who would drive up the rent. The money also was to be used to build affordable housing on city-owned

---

20   "Housing Nashville," Office of the Mayor Megan Barry, https://www.nashville.gov/Portals/0/SiteContent/MayorsOffice/AffordableHousing/Housing%20Nashville%20FINAL.pdf.

property.[21]

Nashville needs economic and cultural diversity in its neighborhoods, the housing report said, calling on citizens to join the government's efforts and to adopt an attitude of YIMBY, meaning "yes in my back yard."

Denver

Denver has been enjoying mile-high growth for years now as a hub for business, technology, and innovation. Fifteen major companies opened center city offices there in 2017 alone, and they brought plenty of jobs. The city's unemployment rate in 2018 was 2.8 percent, one of the lowest in the country.

Along with that growth has come a population boom. From 2010 to 2018, the city grew by 100,000 people, and the downtown workforce grew 20 percent to more than 130,000 people, according to the Downtown Denver Partnership's report for 2018.[22] More than 80,000 people live in the center city area, and nearly 23,000 of them live downtown. The report pointed out that the downtown population had tripled since the turn of the millennium, attributing that growth to people's desire to live in vibrant, walkable neighborhoods near their jobs.

So just who are those folks living downtown? Here's a snapshot: 68 percent have a bachelor's degree or higher, and 78 percent are single without families. Their average age is thirty-four, and their household income averages $120,000.

Every day, more than thirty people move to Denver, looking

21   Joey Garrison, "Nashville Council Approves Barry's $288M Spending Plan, Boosts Bikeway Funding," *Tennessean*, June 14, 2017, https://www.tennessean.com/story/news/2017/06/14/nashville-council-approves-barrys-288-m-spending-plan-boosts-bikeway-funding/395827001/.

22   "2018 State of Downtown Denver Report," Downtown Denver Partnership, https://www.downtowndenver.com/reports/2018-state-downtown-denver-report/.

for a place to call home. The partnership reported that one-bedroom apartments downtown go for an average of $1,734 and for $1,462 throughout the center city neighborhoods. Despite a wave of apartment construction downtown, there still was only one apartment for every six jobs. The city needs to create more affordable housing to meet the demands of the market, the partnership emphasized.

Acknowledging that incomes overall have not kept up with steadily rising housing costs, the city council in 2016 approved Denver's first dedicated housing fund, providing $150 million over ten years to create and preserve affordable housing. The source of the funding is a fee imposed on developers. Two years later, the city adopted a five-year strategy and investment plan to promote affordable housing. The city aims to increase the supply by supporting land-use incentives, expanding the development of accessory dwelling units, using public land to develop affordable housing, and by exploring land trusts.

The five-year strategy, called Housing an Inclusive Denver, centers on four main goals:

→ To create more affordable housing in "inclusive" communities and preserve the affordable housing that already exists.

→ To promote communities that provide opportunities, with good homes, jobs, schools, transportation, and health services.

→ To serve residents with a range of incomes, including the homeless, people on fixed incomes, and working families.

→ To encourage diverse neighborhoods that are welcoming to all.

The plan for 2018 through 2023 calls for investing 40 to 50 percent of the housing resources to help the homeless or people who are earning less than 30 percent of the area's median income. Of those resources, 20 to 30 percent will serve renters earning between 30 and 80 percent of the median, and 20 to 30 percent will go to help residents trying to buy a home or stay in their home. Mayor Michael Hancock praised the strategies as a reflection of the city's values and its desire to lift up its residents who most need support.

CARROTS AND STICKS

It is important to understand the difference between a carrot approach, which offers incentives to encourage developers to participate in affordable housing programs, and a stick approach that mandates participation. The number-one issue with housing affordability is the lack of supply of housing. In our free market economy, if a city's stick is too painful, developers are free to go to another town to build their next projects. Urban policies have a long history of driving developers away with many kinds of sticks, including rent control, inclusionary zoning, and parking minimum mandates.

> **In our free market economy, if a city's stick is too painful, developers are free to go to another town to build their next projects.**

Rent control is a prime example. A *Forbes* magazine article at the turn of the millennium rated rent control as one of the "ten dumbest ideas of the century" in economics.[23] From New York to Hanoi, the policy had harmed cities, the article said. Few economists believe rent control

23   Dan Seligman, "Dumbest Ideas of the Century," *Forbes*, Dec 27, 1999, https://www.forbes.com/forbes/1999/1227/6415094a.html#4df87905f6a3.

makes sense. It discourages investment in housing, thereby stanching the supply of available units. And as demand outstrips supply, many landlords don't feel inclined to keep up with maintenance, particularly in poorer neighborhoods. The older housing stock is eventually lost forever to decay. Municipal leaders need policies that will save those buildings, sometimes called NOAH, or Naturally Occurring Affordable Housing. Rent control isn't going to do that. In fact, real estate investors tend to run if anyone is even whispering that rent control might be a good idea. Why take the risk? Still, where it exists, few city leaders have been willing to speak out against it—although one politician in Hanoi said the artificially low rents had hurt housing more than the American bombers.

Inclusionary zoning, which requires a certain number of affordable housing units in every project, is another policy that can scare away developers. Inclusionary zoning drives up the overall cost of a development, which in turn lessens the desirability for new development and increases the required return on the units that weren't set aside. This increase in the price results in examples such as in New York City, where a construction project will have mostly super luxury units with some token set-aside units. The cost of inclusionary zoning is often such that developers cannot justify building moderate-rate housing options that would be appropriate for most of the population.

Elimination of parking mandates would turn a stick into a carrot for developers. The impact that parking costs have on the construction of housing is one of the greatest barriers to housing affordability. The additional cost for parking requires a new development to charge higher rents in order to secure financing, which is why most of the new construction today is catered to the most affluent renters.

In an op-ed piece in the *Charlotte Observer*, I recently stated that to build a three-hundred-unit apartment community in downtown Charlotte with parking would cost me $75 million, but it would cost only $60 million without parking. That would reduce rent for each resident by over $250 a month, or by about $3,000 a year. In addition, when land must be used to accommodate parking, developers can't build as many apartments. I recently sat in on a series of presentations by the students graduating from Tulane University's Master of Science in Real Estate Sustainability program. One of the projects presented was a seventy-unit development with seven affordable housing units and fifty-four parking spaces. By reducing the required parking to thirty-three spaces, the developer could free up enough land to build ninety units. That could achieve the same economic return while providing seventeen affordable housing units instead of the original seven. It's a matter of scale: rents need to be higher when a landlord must depend on fewer residents to pull in the necessary cash flow to cover fixed costs like land.

Our society is moving away from the car culture. With the increasing popularity of Uber and similar services and the advent of driverless cars, we likely will see a reduced need for parking facilities in the years ahead. And more and more people prefer to hop on their bikes these days. Or they take the train, or the bus. Case in point: a 2016 study by University of Michigan researchers found that only about a quarter of sixteen-year-olds had a driver's license, down from nearly half in 1984.[24] The study identified the trend among all age groups, but particularly among young people in their teens and twenties.

It's all part of the same picture: people want to live where they

24   Michael Sivak and Brandon Schoettle, "Recent Decreases in the Proportion of Persons with a Driver's License across All Age Groups," University of Michigan Transportation Research Institute, Jan 2016, http://www.umich.edu/~umtriswt/PDF/UMTRI-2016-4.pdf.

have easy access to their jobs and to urban services, conveniences, and entertainment. They don't want to waste a large portion of their life stuck in traffic. They want to live near the action. This is no small matter. Americans typically spend 13 percent of their earnings on automobile expenses.[25] They are tired of the costs and hassles of owning and driving a car. If the municipal leaders ignore that trend and continue to cater to car culture, they risk their communities not being attractive in the future. One of the best things a city can do to encourage affordable housing is to provide alternative means of transportation to eliminate the costly need for parking.

In the end, developers are similar to rivers: they will choose the path of least resistance. Sticks often backfire, which is why carrots are often more successful. With the right incentives, I believe many

With the right incentives, I believe many developers will voluntarily include affordable housing in their projects.

developers will voluntarily include affordable housing in their projects.

The affordable housing issue comes down simply to supply and demand. We don't have enough supply to meet the demand, and therefore we should be creating incentives to attract developers instead of giving them excuses to build elsewhere.

We need those incentives now. If prices seem unaffordable today, imagine what the next five years will bring. Millennials are having a huge impact on housing demand and household formations. At the same time, baby boomers are downsizing, creating additional competition for smaller urban housing options. Meanwhile, the United States witnessed an unprecedent

25 "Consumer Expenditures—2018," U.S. Bureau of Labor Statistics Economic News Release, Sept 10, 2019, https://www.bls.gov/news.release/cesan.nr0.htm.

number of births between 1990 and 2007. More and more young people, who typically rent, will be entering adulthood well into the middle of the 2030s. Our housing crisis is just getting started, and it will become increasingly critical over the next fifteen years.

EMBRACING THE FUTURE

Small towns were the fundamental economic units prior to WWII. Today, metropolitan areas have become the new economic power-houses, competing in the world for resources—investment, labor, residents, etc. Towns need to realign themselves with this reality, recognizing that they must define their roles as part of a metropolitan team.

In the late 1980s, the town of Rock Hill, south of Charlotte, had seen thirteen of fourteen textile mills close; a quarter of the employable residents lacked jobs. The downtown was nearly vacant. Rock Hill's economic development strategy at the time was to attract Belk to the downtown mall (which had been created by building a roof over the sides of Main Street, much like the one in Allentown, Pennsylvania) and to recruit industries such as ball bearing plants.

Eventually, Rock Hill embraced a new vision, recognizing that it was now a twenty-mile ring city to the Charlotte metropolitan region. It had underrecognized assets like Winthrop University (the single largest employer besides the city/county at the time) and the Catawba River. Rock Hill ended up taking the roof off the downtown and creating incentives for historic renovation. It created a new civic gateway to the city along David Lyle Blvd.; created a new modern high-tech industrial development park (Waterford) in a joint venture with Childress Klein Properties; initiated the river district redevelopment of over six thousand acres; and started advertising to industry that the town was the "Leading Edge of Charlotte" with access to all of the regional assets (airport, downtown, sports, etc.) and the amenities of a historic town on the river. In a major coup, the town acquired two Masonic columns from a building torn down in downtown Charlotte and incorporated them into their gateway project.

Today, Rock Hill is one of the most successful cities in the Charlotte region. The repositioning effort has attracted tons of quality residential development to York and Lancaster counties. Meanwhile, Winthrop has become a full public university with more than six thousand students.

The point of the story is to illustrate that cities have to: 1) define their position and role in the metropolitan economy; 2) establish a plan for how they can fill that role; 3) establish the policies to encourage actions that support the plan and discourage actions that undermine it; and 4) make the investments to get there. It is really about product development—and the product is the whole metro area. A city or submarket has the opportunity to play a unique role to help attract resources—investment, jobs, people.

I think back to my boyhood in Lexington. Sure, there were ambitious young people in that town and quite an assortment of talent, and yet many of them set their sights only on the furniture factory that had been good to so many for so long. And then it wasn't. By the time I was heading off to college, a lot of my classmates were getting disillusioned about their prospects in a dying town. Some who went off to get a higher education might have come back as entrepreneurs to help the town meet its challenges—but what did Lexington have to offer them in return?

Where there is opportunity, the people will come, and when they come, they will need a place to call home. They will want to live where they can make a good living and improve themselves—if they can afford it. Today, urban economies are providing the greatest opportunity for that economic mobility, but time is of the essence. Urban leaders must understand that what isn't growing is dying.

Where there is opportunity, the people will come, and when they come, they will need a place to call home.

Once a community gains a reputation for success and vibrancy, that reputation propels it even further. Silicon Valley, for example, became a high-tech mecca. The questions up front must always be: How can we attract people? How can we attract employers? Once you get those snowballs rolling, the momentum becomes almost unstoppable.

The formula is not all that complicated. Employers want to see an available, qualified workforce. People want to see available, qualified employers. Success comes to the cities that lift their citizenry, providing support, opportunities for education and training, and decent places to live. Employers take notice and set down stakes—and that attracts more people who in turn will be looking for those decent places to live. Give folks what they need, at a price they can afford, and they will settle down to stay.

Communities that give developers the most trouble will attract the least talented ones. Time is money, and a day's delay can be costly. The best developers go where they can find a better opportunity and where the atmosphere is conducive to everyone's growth. Communities that welcome developers will attract the best developers and, hence, the best projects.

Chapel Hill, for example, faces an affordability shortage and crisis—and yet many developers have stayed away. The town's permitting process is beyond onerous. It is unpredictable, which makes it too risky for a shrewd developer to take such a gamble. By contrast, the neighboring town of Durham has seen a dramatic change in its downtown and its tax base because of its welcoming approach. The goal is to find a balance. As attitudes have been changing in Chapel Hill, town officials have been working hard to improve the commercial tax base. The progressive mayor has helped townspeople to understand the importance of growth in core neighborhoods while still protecting the surrounding farmland.

Green buffers around a city are a nice aesthetic touch with environmental benefits. Portland, Oregon, has one, and Chapel Hill too. Open space improves the quality of life. In the core of a city, though, urban leaders must be careful about imposing burdensome development limits. They shouldn't try to have it both ways: if they want to keep things green around the city perimeter, they need to encourage development within. At the end of the day, an open field will always be the cheapest place to build, but considering the resulting costs for such things as roads, sewer systems, fire and police services, and garbage collection, not to mention the ordeal of traffic jams, it may prove the most costly place in the long run.

City life is simply more efficient—and responsible leaders should be looking for efficient growth to meet the rising demand for housing. A multifamily building is far more cost-efficient than a single-family house. For example, in Charlotte, the cost to pick up trash at an apartment is less than one-third of the cost to pick up trash from a single-family home. This is just one of hundreds of reasons why municipalities should be welcoming apartments.

Today apartment life is not just for the cash-strapped. People who can afford an expensive house in a suburban subdivision don't necessarily want to live in one. Urban leaders should pay attention to the demographic trends: many of the millennials and boomers as well as others want to live in the cities these days. They want to go where they can find opportunity and excitement. They want to avoid wasting their life stuck in commuter traffic. The cities that thrive in the twenty-first century will be those that accommodate the urban dreamers who want to invest their money into more than just another tank of gas.

CHAPTER 7

THE OPPORTUNITY

> Ideas are important, but they're not essential. What's essential and important is the execution of the idea.
>
> **John Landis**

IN THE WANING DAYS of the Second World War, Abraham Levitt and his two sons looked out on the potato and onion fields about thirty miles east of New York City and envisioned a crop of simple houses, row upon row. There they conceived Levittown, the planned community that has come to symbolize suburbia and the picket fence dream. By the late 1940s, their company was building thirty houses a day for the families of GIs back from the battlefields of Europe and the Pacific and eager to settle down.

The Levitts saw an opportunity, cashed in, and expanded their brand, and soon they were operating one of the largest home construction companies in the United States. In doing so, they helped to meet a huge demand for affordable suburban housing. Today, our society struggles with a similarly large demand for affordable urban housing. Our challenge, and our opportunity, is to seize the moment and do it right—this time by finding a way to make the American Dream accessible for everyone.

For a decade before the war, Levitt & Sons had been custom designing and building expensive homes, just a few hundred a year, for upper-middle-class families on Long Island. During the war, the housing industry stagnated, with little new residential construction except for defense contracts near military facilities. Labor and materials were in short supply. In the best of times, few could afford to buy a custom home. In wartime, even the wealthy waited.

One of the sons, William, served in the Seabees construction battalion of the Navy and learned firsthand how the military erected structures quickly and inexpensively using standardized materials. That's the way to go, he told his father and brother Alfred, an architect. Mass production had revolutionized the auto industry. The housing industry needed something similar. The company had gained some practical experience in the mass construction of housing for naval personnel in the Norfolk, Virginia, area. Now, with the war over, it was time to adapt those skills to serve the pressing need for private housing.

The Levitts designed a few variations of a modest Cape Cod-style house of one floor with an unfinished attic, which they marketed as expansion space. They shipped in loads of precut lumber from their own timberland and mill on the West Coast. Subcontractors moved from house to house, each completing a single task in a twenty-six-step construction process with assembly-line efficiency. The local officials allowed the homes to be built on slabs of concrete instead of basement foundations. The need for affordable homes was too critical to quibble.

In postwar America, communities nationwide faced a housing crisis. The years of fighting were over. It was time now to get on with living. This was the beginning of the car culture, and many young families looked to suburbia for a place they could afford. They didn't find much at first. The demand overran the supply by far. "Any damn fool can build homes," said William Levitt, who took control of the company in 1954. "What counts is how many you can sell for how little." Many consider him the father of modern suburbia in the United States and the Henry Ford of the housing industry.

At first, the Levitts assembled rental homes, and tenants snapped them up. Soon the company was offering the homes for sale, starting at $8,000 (which had the buying power of about $94,000 in 2019 dollars). Then, in the Housing Act of 1949, the federal government greatly expanded FHA mortgage insurance. The Veterans Administration also offered loan guarantees. With those incentives, many buyers could get into a home for only $400 down. It was a price point that stimulated even greater demand.

Levitt & Sons went on to build a total of more than seventeen thousand homes in the Long Island community, each with about 750 square feet of space. Later the company began selling a somewhat larger ranch house—five models with minor variations—in response to those who criticized the development as humdrum in its uniformity.

Then, in the early 1950s, the company expanded to Pennsylvania, where it recognized another big opportunity. It purchased nearly six thousand acres northeast of Philadelphia, and soon the fields of broccoli and spinach were giving way to rows of houses in a second Levittown. The houses filled quickly. Two miles away, the US Steel Corp. had broken ground for its Fairless Hills plant. Thousands of workers would need convenient and affordable housing close to work. Levitt & Sons rushed to meet the demand, continuing to build there until 1958. This encore Levittown, like the first, grew to more than seventeen thousand simple homes, but this time included an assortment of six styles.

Onward to New Jersey where, ten miles to the south and across the Delaware River, the company purchased almost the entire rural township of Willingboro. There, starting in 1958, it would build eleven thousand homes with an easy commute to Philadelphia, Trenton, and Camden. This time, the company offered a mix of housing types at different prices, aiming to attract wealthier home-owners as neighbors to working-class buyers. Next door to the modest Cape Cods and ranchers, fancier colonials popped up. By building within a single municipality, the company avoided the mishmash of zoning regulations and building codes that had dogged it in Pennsylvania. And so yet another Levittown was born, although the residents voted five years later to go back to the old name. To have two communities with the same name so close together caused too much confusion.

TUNED IN, TUNED OUT

Such was the trajectory of a company that was tuned in to oppor-tunity. Levitt & Sons knew what folks wanted. They did more than build and sell houses. They sold the dream. They planned com-munities and created neighborhoods. The master plans for their developments included schools, churches, shopping centers, public swimming pools, and ballfields. This was the full suburban package, set into place and assembled in pieces.

Standing at the forefront of significant changes in society, the Levitt family made a lot of money. So did many others at the time who recognized the housing shortage and who stepped in as entrepreneurs and investors, working together to meet the acute demand. Many developers replicated the mass production model, producing fifteen million units nationwide by the end of the 1950s. Levitt & Sons, which launched the movement, provided the opportunity for tens of thousands of families to become first-time homeowners and find their American Dream.

Tens of thousands of others did not. For years, African Americans were unwelcome in the homogenous zone of the Levittowns, which to many also became a symbol of racial segregation. "We can solve the housing problem or we can solve the racial problem, but we cannot combine the two," William Levitt said.[26] Even if he recognized the inequity, he chose to tune it out so as not to wreck the investment.

It was a problem that indeed ran deep. The FHA and the Veterans Administration for years endorsed the practice of redlining, so called because of the color code on federal maps indicating regions where black families either lived or were living nearby. The Housing Act of 1949 claimed that its goal was "a decent home and suitable living environment for every American family"—except not really. The FHA's underwriting manual would not insure loans to black families, asserting that "incompatible racial groups should not be permitted to live in the same communities."

William Levitt instructed his agents to accept no applications from African Americans, including veterans. The contracts prohibited buyers from renting or allowing the use of the property by anyone except Caucasians. That's not discrimination, he insisted. That's good business—because, after all, he was only trying to protect the value of the investment. "As a Jew, I have no room in my mind or heart for racial prejudice. But the plain fact is that most whites prefer not to

---

26   Quoted in Joshua Ruff, "For Sale: The American Dream," *American History* 42, no.5 (December 2007): 42-49.

live in mixed communities. This attitude may be wrong morally, and someday it may change. I hope it will."[27] Nonetheless, the company at first resisted selling to Jews, too, but later relented; and then, in 1957, a Jewish couple in the Pennsylvania community arranged to resell their house to a black family.

On the day that William and Daisy Myers and their sons moved in, the mailman went door to door announcing, "It's happened! It's happened!" Neighbors proceeded to torment the couple. Each evening, a jeering mob gathered outside their house, throwing rocks. A court order prohibited more than three people from assembling near the residence at once, but the Levittown police failed to enforce it. The Ku Klux Klan burned a cross and painted epithets on the house. One neighbor renamed his black dog after one of those epithets and took every opportunity to loudly call for it.

Other white families, however, came to the Myerses' defense and aid, organizing a citizen patrol and helping them with babysitting and household chores. After two weeks, the state police came in to quell the riots, but the harassment continued for months. The state attorney general eventually intervened to stop a "malicious and evil conspiracy" and prosecuted the ringleaders of the Levittown Betterment Community, which they had established for the sole purpose of driving out the family. But the damage was done. After a few years, the family moved out, discouraged but not bitter. Daisy and Bill Myers were careful to point out that the experience had shown them the best in people, not just the worst.

Change was beginning. Still, it would be years before the rulings of the civil rights movement of the 1950s and '60s had much effect on the complexion of the Levittowns.

27   Quoted in David Kushner, *Levittown: Two Families, One Tycoon, and the Fight for Civil Rights in America's Legendary Suburb* (New York: Walker, 2009).

Levitt & Sons had solutions to the housing shortage of the time. Their business model was an investor's dream of fast, efficient construction that kept costs down while meeting a booming demand. Opportunity beckoned—first, to serve the young postwar families, and then to house the factory workers in a rapidly industrializing America. Meanwhile, the baby boom was in full force. In the years to come, it would continue to fuel the demand.

Levitt & Sons tried to engineer communities down to the details of what they saw as the perfect suburban ecosystem. Hoping to establish the intimacy of neighborhoods, they laid out networks of streets and carefully located playgrounds and civic centers. They understood that to cash in on this huge opportunity, they needed to please the people. They just didn't include all the people. The result: an unbalanced, unhealthy ecosystem. When you leave a lot of folks out, when you circle them off the map, do you really have a community at all?

I know how my father would have answered that question. After all, he started Grubb Properties in defiance of the redlining practice that left folks out. And I know his approach is the right one.

VALUE IS ALWAYS IN VOGUE

Let's turn again to the example of Glen Lennox, conceived and built about the same time as the first Levittown. It has become the kind of real, diverse community where people can dream and grow. It, too, was built to meet a severe postwar housing shortage as veterans poured into Chapel Hill, eager to attend the University of North Carolina on the GI Bill.

Today, Glen Lennox continues to grow on the value of a great location. The university has consistently been ranked number one by *US News and World Report* for the best value of any university.

Meanwhile, Glen Lennox has consistently been a powerful investment since Grubb Properties purchased it in 1985, near the peak of that decade's real estate bubble. In the real estate recession of the late 1980s and early '90s, the community's occupancy rate never dropped below 93 percent, and it posted annual revenue growth in that period of 5.5 percent. It repeated a big spike in income during the tech bust of 2000 and 2001; and during the Great Recession its net income continued to rise. In fact, its net income from 2008 to 2010 rose by over 25 percent.

Those were tough times for the overall housing industry, but Glen Lennox did more than endure. It thrived. During a major economic downturn, what do people do? They go back to school. Where do they go? To the school that offers the greatest value for the money. And where do they live? At a place like Glen Lennox, which also offers great value for the money.

Affordable housing in a great location will perform well even in the worst of times.

When you are delivering what the market needs, you will continue to do well through the decades. Affordable housing in a great location will perform well even in the worst of times, and the indexes show that multifamily housing consistently outperforms any other asset class in real estate. In other words, investing in value-based multifamily housing is typically a safe bet. As one of my board members put it: "In real estate, the office developers live better, but the multifamily developers sleep better."

As with any real estate investment, location is key. A good location with affordable rents will attract a broader range of tenants, reducing risk significantly. Most people in the industry believe that real estate tracks the Consumer Price Index and see it as a hedge against inflation, but I believe it tracks the earning power of the neighborhood where it is located. Wherever people are getting good salaries and raises, properties should enjoy decent rental increases, too.

Our society's demand for affordable housing will not cease during our lifetimes. After World War II, developers met the demand by building homes in suburban settings and getting the construction down to an efficient science, reducing the price of what ordinary folks had to pay to either rent or own. Today, Grubb Properties is striving to meet the demand in urban settings with its Link Apartments multi-family housing developments. We have designed desirable apartment communities that we can replicate in city after city. We offer two floor plans designed specifically to allow folks making as little as 60 percent of the median income to live without overburdening their housing costs as a percentage of their income.

Glen Lennox is a great example of a community that has come full circle: when it was built, it was suburban, but today it has become an urban oasis. We are redeveloping it in a thoughtful manner to attract smart people with promising futures.

We have set a goal of making sure that 50 percent of the commutes to and from Glen Lennox by 2030 are by some form of transportation other than the automobile. In his 2010 book *The Great Reset*, Richard Florida reported that commuting was wasting 4.2 billion hours of work time annually across the United States, or nearly a full workweek for every commuter. The overall cost to the US economy was nearly $90 billion when lost productivity and wasted fuel were taken into account. This doesn't even count the amount of money wasted on parking. The institute calculated that shaving off just one minute from the average commute time would save the US economy $19.5 billion, he wrote. Fifteen minutes would save $292 billion. Adjusting for inflation since his book was published, those figures would be 15 percent higher in 2019.

Today we have close to 2 billion parking spaces in America for approximately 250 million cars, an eight-to-one ratio.[28] Eric Scharnhorst did a study for the Research Institute for Housing America on the impact of parking in five cities.[29] The study determined that New York has 1.85 million parking spaces, which is only about 0.6 of a space per household and 10 spaces per acre. While parking replacement there is the most expensive per space, the average cost of parking replacement was only $6,570 per household, an efficient number.

Wasted resources spent on excess parking and commute times are destroying America's competitive advantage globally and dramatically impacting economic mobility for the majority of the population.

On the other hand, Seattle has 1.6 million parking spaces and 5.2 spaces per household and its average cost of parking was $117,000 per household—a dramatically higher amount, due to the sheer excess number of spaces. Jackson Hole, Wyoming, was even worse. It has 27 parking spaces per household, resulting in a parking cost of $192,000 per household. Although those numbers probably are missing some components of construction prices for different types of parking spaces, the overall point is crystal clear: wasted resources spent on excess parking and commute times are destroying America's competitive advantage globally and dramatically impacting economic mobility for the majority of the population.

28   Laura Bliss, "America Probably Has Enough Parking Spaces for Multiple Black Fridays," CityLab, Nov 27, 2018, https://www.citylab.com/transportation/2018/11/parking-lots-near-me-shopping-plazas-vacant-spaces/576646/.

29   Eric Scharnhorst, "Quantified Parking: Comprehensive Parking Inventories for Five US Cities," Research Institute for Housing America Special Report, May 2018.

In Charlotte, NC, where I live, if you have to change buses on the way to work, the average commute time is 90 minutes. If that commuter were able to work that extra three hours a day at just $10/hour, that would result in $7,500 of additional earnings. Sadly, wasted time spent commuting is a typical obstacle to folks who need to work in urban areas but cannot afford to live there.

Recently, the McColl Center for Visual Arts in Charlotte, one of the country's premier artist-in-residency programs, secured a $400,000 grant to work with homeless people and artists to have a positive impact on North Tryon, Charlotte's main street. I assisted in helping the center secure the grant and served on the committee to implement it. I was assigned to work with a committee member, Eveco, on a photo image display. We were asked to bring something that reminded us of North Tryon. Eveco brought a "crack can" she had found on the street—a soft drink can that someone had turned into a crack pipe. I brought my keys. The night before, I had locked myself out of my condominium and called Pic-a-Lock—and $110 later, I was back in my condo a half block off of North Tryon. The locksmith hadn't even asked for my ID. I am certain that Eveco would not have gotten the same treatment, given she was an African American female who had recently been homeless.

Together we got an impressive collection of pictures and I did my first Instagram posting, which can be found at #createnorthtryon. And I had the privilege of getting to know Eveco and learn more about her story. She had been laid off from UPS five years previously. Eventually, her money ran out and she became homeless. She now lived at Moore House, a transitional housing project. Eveco was not crazy about living there due to the drug use of many of its occupants. However, she was thankful for the hand up and had recently secured a job paying a little over $8.50 an hour. Her shift started at 9 p.m.

Pictures from my #createnorthtryon Instagram posting, including the "crack can."

She left Moore House around 6:00 each night, catching a bus to the main bus terminal in downtown Charlotte. From there she hopped on the light rail system, which took her out to a stop about ten miles away. Then she caught an additional bus from the light rail station to a stop a few blocks from her work. If all went smoothly, she would arrive at 8:35 with twenty-five minutes to relax before work.

At one of our morning meetings, Eveco told me that she had come there straight from her job. She had worked all night and then voluntarily attended our workshop. At that moment, it became clearer than ever to me how challenging our society makes life for so many. Here was someone commuting two and a half hours to a job paying less than ten dollars an hour. How can we expect someone to move up the economic ladder under those conditions? And this was happening in the wealthy, progressive city of Charlotte.

It's ludicrous—but there is hope if we not only improve mass transit but also focus on developing more affordable urban housing so people can live near their jobs, and ideally even take a bike to work. As the world becomes more urban, it is high time to seize that opportunity.

A RAPIDLY URBANIZING SOCIETY

We are a rapidly urbanizing society. Around the world, three million people are moving into cities every week in search of a better life. Today, 54 percent of the planet's population live in urban areas, a proportion that has nearly doubled since 1950. By 2050, it will be approaching 70 percent.

Those figures come from Robert Muggah, a Canadian political scientist and widely cited authority on urban issues. "Cities are where the future happens first," he says. "They're open, they're creative, they're dynamic, they're democratic, they're cosmopolitan, they're sexy." If you live in a city, "you're likely to be healthier, wealthier, better educated, and live longer than your country cousins."[30]

In the United States, the urban population eclipsed the rural population in the 1920 census and has grown steadily every decade since. The figure for 2018 was 84 percent of the population living in urban areas, and the trend continues. That's a trajectory that poses serious challenges our society must solve. As Richard Florida explains, "The outflow of the less affluent is especially troubling, because urban centers offer both better job opportunities and greater levels of the kinds of amenities that can help boost wages and increase prospects for economic mobility … in fact the prospects for upward economic mobility are substantially worse in less populated, more spread out metros, where the disadvantaged tend to be located farther away from jobs and economic opportunities." The primary challenge is the need for affordable housing where economic opportunities are greatest.

I believe this is where the investment and banking community can have a real impact. As I was quoted in the *Charlotte Observer* in

---

30   Robert Muggah, "The Biggest Risks Facing Cities—and Some Solutions," TED, https://www.ted.com/talks/robert_muggah_ the_biggest_risks_facing_cities_and_some_solutions/ transcript?language=en.

2000 and still feel is true today, I do not believe the housing industry can overbuild our urban areas. We can price people out of them, and that is what has been happening, but if we can provide safe, secure affordable housing, the demand is virtually unlimited. But the challenge is great. For example, in the San Francisco and Los Angeles urban regions, a typical home costs ten times the average annual income. What safer investment exists than urban housing that is affordable? Fortunately, much of the investment community is starting to appreciate the security of investments in apartments.

A NEW MINDSET FOR HOUSING

While I've touched on a range of opportunities to improve housing affordability, the issue really requires a broader disconnection from the traditional process of housing production that has largely been the approach in America since World War II. This is what I call the "frontier mindset." Like the frontier days of America, this approach views resources such as land, infrastructure, labor, and raw materials as abundant. As a result, decisions about land use, density, roads, utilities, surface parking, and other components of housing production are thought of independently with an emphasis on expediency and initial cost.

The reality is that all of these inputs have become considerably more scarce and expensive, resulting in an average cost of new single-family housing today reaching close to $400,000 per home and the average cost for an apartment unit reaching close to $200,000. The total cumulative housing production shortfall is over 3.5 million units.[31] What was once America's greatest advantage—abundance of land at low cost—has eroded, replaced instead with scarcity and cost inputs rising at a pace well above inflation. According to the Joint

31   Peter Linneman, *The Linneman Letter*, vol. 18, issue 2, Summer 2018.

Center for Housing Studies at Harvard University, the United States has now dropped to eleventh of the top twelve developed countries in rental affordability (measured as housing cost to income).[32] Only Spain was lower. At the same time, the US is in the middle of a fast-changing demand environment with increasing need for entry-level housing types for millennials swelling the workforce ranks, as well as opportunities for aging baby boomers shifting their housing needs.

To make matters worse, because we've largely spent the last seventy years since World War II supporting this pattern of development and housing production, the resulting urban sprawl is now financially unstable. Aging infrastructure will lead to higher taxes as local, state, and federal governments are ultimately required to fund repair and replacements, exacerbating the housing affordability problem in the coming years. Meanwhile, the relatively limited investments in transit and smart growth have not made a dent in the mobility and affordability issues facing Americans. Our country needs a new approach.

Instead of the frontier mindset to housing, our company advocates a "stewardship mindset" based on principles of efficiency. Unlike the frontier mindset, stewardship regards resources as limited and emphasizes ways in which these resources can be stretched, shared, or minimized in order to drive down the effective cost per output unit of housing.

For example, this mindset has led our company to redevelop existing properties in urban or infill locations where road, water, sewer, and stormwater infrastructure is already in place and does not require the significant new infrastructure investments typical of green field development. We also look to pair uses such as office

---

32   Michael Carliner and Ellen Marya, "Rental Housing: An International Comparison," JCHS Research Brief, September 2016, https://www.jchs.harvard.edu/sites/default/files/brief_international_housing_carliner_marya.pdf.

and apartments where parking can be shared efficiently, reducing capital and operating expenses for both property types. We focus on designing extremely efficient housing, providing space where it really matters. This allows us to build units that are one hundred fifty to two hundred square feet smaller than what was built historically, but with better amenities and use of space. For years, we had to design around three-foot-deep televisions, for example. Today's slim TVs allow that space to be put to better use, and many millennials don't want a TV at all. They watch video on their laptops and phones and would not dream of wasting money on a television set.

To be clear, the stewardship approach requires creative thinking and hard work. For example, higher-density zoning can often be controversial in communities, so it takes patient listening and hand-holding with community stakeholders and political leaders to come to consensus. Adaptive reuse of existing properties requires working diligently with lenders on items such as master associations, shared parking easements, and other more complicated legal structures. Smaller housing floor plans means obsessing over design and efficiency, tracking the results over a broad portfolio, and continually refining and testing.

While this type of work can be difficult, it can also be rewarding. Our investors enjoy the benefits of higher returns with lower risk; the cities and counties we work in gain tax base without significant additional infrastructure investments; the communities we partner with gain important workforce housing close to jobs, transportation, and amenities; and the environment is improved by resolving prior development impact on our stream beds and offsetting development that might otherwise be built in forest and farm areas.

The stewardship mindset may require even broader thinking and disruption going forward. America has long been a country of home ownership. It's been part of the DNA of the country from the founding of the colonies to the post-World War II housing boom when national policy, regulations, financing, and investments were hyper-allocated to support home ownership. This resulted in record home ownership levels peaking at 68 percent in 2007. But it also resulted in market manipulation and even corruption, as became evident in the 2008–2009 global financial crisis and economic recession. The finance machine built to support this housing model—and too often take advantage of it—broke.

Rental housing over those seventy years since World War II has struggled for acceptance based on the perception that it is an inferior class of housing. Although advocacy by rental housing producers and organizations such as National Multifamily Housing Council has sought to change this perception, the broader public policy as well as the semipublic and private financing sources have stacked the deck against it. The reality is that rental housing is a fundamentally important tool in getting to affordability overall. Other countries around the world have a more balanced allocation of home ownership and rental housing.

In summary, if we want to help folks like Eveco, it will take a new mindset to tackle the problem of housing affordability. This means a new approach to resources and a broader view of the role that different types of housing should play in our future. The American housing landscape will need to change if it hopes to be competitive in the world marketplace. We will need to transform the traditional formulas for how we design, fund, build, regulate, and market housing solutions. Seizing this opportunity will require creative thinking, willingness to work hard, and an open mindset to possibilities.

CHAPTER 8

THE LONG VIEW

▌ *Simplicity is the shortest path to a solution.*

Ward Cunningham

THE ROOFS LEAKED, THE soffits were rotting, and mold had spread in the tiny apartments that lacked air conditioning—but those were just a few of the outward signs of a deeper level of decay in the Boulevard Homes neighborhood of west Charlotte.

Built in 1970, the three-hundred-unit public housing project had descended into worsening poverty and crime, becoming one of the city's most troubled neighborhoods. Today, it is an exciting neighborhood where hope prevails—and a model for affordable housing that could transform many communities in the years ahead. It represents a vision of what can be if we embrace progressive strategies that put people first.

In 2010, the Charlotte Housing Authority was weighing whether to fix up the thirty-four-acre site or to bulldoze it and start anew. The statistics there were grim: the median household income was $14,076, way below the citywide median of $52,148. Ninety-three percent of the residents received food stamps. In only a fifth of the households did anyone have a job. Teen pregnancies were about three times higher than the city's overall rate, and high schoolers were about three times more likely to drop out. Violent crime in the development was five times higher than the city average.[33]

Boulevard Homes' day was done. The housing authority decided to raze all the buildings and received a $20.9 million federal grant through the Hope VI program of HUD for redevelopment. The authority committed up to $9 million in funding, and the city of Charlotte contributed $12 million in voter-approved funds. In all, the project was expected to total $90 million and include investments from HUD, the housing authority, the school district, and the city, as well as tax credits, bank financing, and philanthropy. The stakeholders involved wanted to replace this failed old housing project with something far better.

The result was Renaissance West, a modern community of 334 brick apartments and townhomes connected by wide sidewalks lined with shade trees and lamps. No longer a bleak parcel of poverty, this is now a bright spot where anyone can live and everyone can succeed. Some residents pay full rent at the market rate, while others get subsidies with the stipulation that they must work, go to school, or get career training for at least thirty hours a week. About a third of the apartments were set aside for seniors age sixty-five or over or for disabled residents. The planners took great care to ensure a smooth transition for the existing residents of Boulevard Homes.

In the spirit of rebuilding lives as well as the landscape, the Renaissance West development includes an education village and offers supportive services for families. The neighborhood's corner-

33   "Charlotte Neighborhood Quality of Life Study 2010 and Business Corridor Bench-marking Analysis," Metropolitan Studies Group, University of North Carolina at Charlotte, September 13, 2010, https://charlottenc.gov/HNS/CE/CommunityInfo/Documents/2010%20Quality%20Of%20Life%20Report.pdf.

stone is a K–8 charter school. At the childhood development center, little kids get off to a good start in school and in life. For adults, a community center offers job training, GED classes, counseling on financial and computer literacy, and more. Residents have easy access to youth and adult programs and to health and wellness services.

The nonprofit Renaissance West Community Initiative, or RWCI, organized to coordinate those educational and service offerings. Its "cradle-to-career" approach tackles the many issues that keep families in poverty—whether it's a lack of education, skills, childcare, and transportation or their struggles with crime, substance abuse, and mental health problems.

RWCI embraces the principle that a safe, progressive environment transforms how people view themselves and their neighborhood. When you can replace desperation and fear with pride and possibilities, you are building a new way of life. The goal is to break the cycle of urban poverty from generation to generation. RWCI advanced that cause by joining the Purpose Built Communities network.

As its model for success, Purpose Built Communities points to the East Lake development in Atlanta, which like Boulevard Homes was once an impoverished, violent neighborhood. Today it is a thriving community of high-quality housing for mixed incomes. Violent crime is down 95 percent. The neighborhood school, once Atlanta's worst, today is one of the best in the city and state. East Lake's revival also has boosted the value of nearby homes and attracted substantial investment in residential and commercial development. Success builds on success.

That's the formula that has worked for Renaissance West, whose developer, Laurel Street Residential, is headquartered in Charlotte. The company's president and chief executive officer, Dionne Nelson, is a leader in mixed-income housing and has built such communities throughout the Carolinas and Virginia. Remarkably, the community that Laurel Street built in Charlotte has a unique feature. When folks there find their lives improving as a result of the resources provided to them, they are not forced to pick up stakes and move. Renaissance residents can not only choose to stay in the same neighborhood but to stay in the same apartment. They can sleep with confidence at night knowing the place they call home won't go away if they get a lucky break and improve their employment prospects.

That has seldom been the case under HUD policy, which has a long history of inflexibility: once an apartment had been classified for affordable, subsidized housing, it had to stay that way. HUD policies for many years have been to ship people off once they earn an income too high to qualify them for assistance. This removes role models from the community and forces them to move to unfamiliar neighborhoods where support isn't likely to exist and their relationships aren't as strong, if they exist at all.

Let's say a rental has been set aside for a family making less than 30 percent of the median income for the region. If that family "graduates" to making between 30 and 60 percent, historically HUD policy was they had to move. The family might get a lesser subsidy via a Section 8 voucher that it can use to reduce its rental expenses at another place, out of the community—but the point is, the family gets dislocated from the place it called home. This prohibits any chance for improvement in that particular neighborhood. As a result, residents become more focused on not accidentally improving their lives by earning too much income to avoid traumatic relocation, a perverse concept encouraged by government policy.

To disrupt a neighborhood through forced expulsions is not the answer, even when the neighborhood is troubled. Jane Jacobs, in *The*

Death and Life of Great American Cities (1961), made that clear in her pioneering critique of urban planning policies of the 1950s that she blamed for the decline of city neighborhoods. She championed vibrant, diverse urban communities and opposed slum clearances and "renewal" efforts like the proposed expressway through SoHo and Little Italy in New York City.

For generations, HUD policies have not just been disruptive but downright destructive for so many families. Losing a subsidy feels like a penalty to struggling households who finally are seeing some light, but even worse can be the prospect of having to leave home. Fortunately, HUD is starting to appreciate the problem, and, therefore, that won't happen at Renaissance West. Of the remaining apartments not set aside for seniors and the disabled, one-third are for folks earning less than 30 percent of median income trying to improve their lives, and one-third are for working families earning up to 60 percent. The other third of the households pay their rent at the market rate—still affordable, but unsubsidized. If a family's income rises above 30 percent of the median, it doesn't have to move out. The family can stay in the same apartment while getting a Section 8 subsidy, and still can stay there even if their income rises above the 60 percent mark. Another apartment, when it becomes available, simply is designated for a family that is eligible for available subsidy. This works, given the natural turnover of apartments.

In other words, instead of forcing families to get out, HUD has agreed to simply reclassify the apartments at Renaissance West when necessary—a simple solution, but a big step forward in fostering neighborhood pride and the comfort of home. It's the kind of policy that encourages people to do better in life. It's the kind of policy that makes them want to take better care of their homes, their neighborhoods, and themselves.

That is the model that should gain traction nationwide as other communities observe how well it works, particularly when combined with improvements in education and social services. No one can deny the clear evidence of success when comparing the *before* and *after* of places such as East Lake in Atlanta or Renaissance West in Charlotte. Where once hope was fading, these have become vibrant communities. Unfortunately, we may not be seeing more such examples as HUD, to reduce costs, phases out the Hope VI program.

> **He brought a social consciousness to his endeavors, looking for ways to ensure that his development projects would encourage social interaction and a sense of responsibility to one's community and neighbors.**

A VISION OF WHAT CAN BE

"Whatever ought to be, can be," said James Rouse, the visionary developer who was one of the great humanitarians in the real estate business.[34] The founder of the Rouse Company, he built the model city of Columbia, Maryland, where he envisioned economic, racial, and cultural harmony, and he later launched the Enterprise Foundation, which supports affordable housing and social services in lower-income neighborhoods.

The life and work of Jim Rouse exemplifies much of what our industry can do right. He sought more than profit. He brought a social consciousness to his endeavors, looking for ways to ensure that his development projects would encourage social interaction and a sense of responsibility to one's community and neighbors.

A contemporary of the Levitts and other developers of planned

34   Paul Marx, *Jim Rouse: Capitalist/Idealist* (Maryland: University Press of America, 2007).

communities who accommodated the American flight to the suburbs, Rouse turned his attention back to the cities, "to make them work for the people who live there."[35] Known as an early developer of enclosed shopping malls, he saw their potential in town centers. He developed the Faneuil Hall Marketplace in Boston, which inspired such urban malls as Baltimore's Harborplace and lower Manhattan's South Street Seaport.

Emphasizing residential development that would be affordable and open to all, Rouse aimed "to feed into the city some of the atmosphere and pace of the small town and village" and to encourage "a spirit and feeling of neighborliness and a rich sense of belonging to a community." That was the spirit in which he devoted his retirement years to his nonprofit foundation, which he considered to be his most important work by far. The foundation (now Enterprise Community Partners) has worked with hundreds of municipal groups in developing safe and affordable urban housing, emphasizing access to good schools, jobs, transportation, and health care.[36]

Rouse would be proud of what other visionaries have accomplished in communities like Renaissance West in Charlotte. It's his kind of place. The day should come, he said, when we can lift people out of their need for subsidized housing and give them the opportunity to purchase the homes where they have built their lives. Our society isn't there yet, in most cases, but at least we have great examples where we are pursuing a model that doesn't uproot folks and send them packing just as they are tasting success. We must value human dignity. If we keep our focus on what ought to be, then surely it can be.

---

35   Jimmy Stamp, "James W. Rouse's Legacy of Better Living Through Design," *Smithsonian*, April 23, 2014, https://www.smithsonianmag.com/history/james-w-rouses-legacy-better-living-through-design-180951187/.

36   Marx, *Jim Rouse: Capitalist/Idealist.*

BRIGHTER DAYS AHEAD

The demand for urban housing continues to swell as the millennial generation works its way through the pipeline. As we saw in chapter two, the birth rate hit another peak in 2007, nearly a decade after the last of the millennials were born. Many of those folks won't be renting their first apartment until the early 2030s.

The existing programs and the current pace of construction are insufficient to deal with all the households these young folks will create. Meanwhile, many people from the boomer and Gen X crowd whose nests have emptied, or soon will, are looking to downsize. Deidre and I, for example, just moved downtown into a condominium 40 percent smaller than our house: with our kids away at school, we don't need as much house anymore. As more couples look to downsize, many are attracted to city life. What happens, though, is they are just adding to the demand for a supply that isn't there. As economics 101 taught us, when demand outstrips supply, what was expensive by most people's standards becomes even more unaffordable.

This much is clear: for at least the next ten to fifteen years, the demand for housing will outstrip the supply. That imbalance has the inevitable effect of pushing prices upward. That is why since the turn of the millennium the cost of constructing a new house has grown at three times the overall inflation rate as measured by the Consumer Price Index.

The US homeownership rate (the percentage of homes occupied by the owner) was 64 percent in 2017, according to the Census Bureau, down about four points from a decade earlier.[37] And from

---

37 "Table 17. Homeownership Rates for the United States, by Age of Householder and by Family Status: 1982 to 2017," United States Census Bureau, https://www.census.gov/housing/hvs/files/annual17/ann17t_17.xlsx.

1980 into the new millennium, increasingly few of those homeowners were younger people in their twenties to mid-forties, the statistics
show. In 2006, more than 40 percent of homeowners were under age
thirty-five. Today, they make up less than a third.

There are many reasons for the reduction in homeownership. One
is that couples are marrying later. The other is the desire to maintain
mobility in order to pursue better job opportunities. Between 2006
and 2016, student loan debt increased by 170 percent, according
to the Federal Reserve Bank of New York, and 2015 graduates with
loans left school owing about $34,000—up from only $20,000 ten
years earlier.[38] This debt is forcing more folks out of rural communities where earnings potential is not as great and into urban areas,
where ownership of housing is more expensive. This is also pushing
down homeownership.

As I was writing this, a headline on the front of the *Wall Street
Journal* caught my eye: "The Next Real-Estate Crisis: A Shortage of
New Homes."[39] The newspaper reported that the pace of new home
construction in the United States, in proportion to the population,
was nearly the lowest ever despite the booming economy. A Michigan
home builder told the reporter that demand for reasonably priced
houses was strong but that the doubling of land and construction
costs and the prevailing shortage of labor had forced him to change
his strategy since the mid-2000s. Back then, he built about twenty-
five homes a year, many of them entry-level. Now, he's down to a
dozen, but they are high-end ones because the profit margin is too

38 "2017 Press Briefing: Household Borrowing, Student Debt Trends and Homeowner-
    ship," Federal Reserve Bank of New York, https://www.newyorkfed.org/press/press-
    briefings/household-borrowing-student-loans-homeownership; Courtney Connley, "A
    New Study Says an Overwhelming Majority of Millennials Want to Be Homeowners,
    but Student Loans Are Holding Them Back," *CNBC*, Dec 8 2018, https://www.cnbc.
    com/2018/12/08/student-loan-burden-barring-millenials-from-home-ownership-
    study.html.

39 Laura Kusisto, *Wall Street Journal*, Page A1, March 19, 2018.

small for less expensive homes for him to justify building.

Nationwide, it's a similar story: construction isn't keeping pace with rising demand. The inventory of new and existing homes for sale hit a record low in 2017, according to the National Association of Realtors.

So what are young people to do if they expect to live somewhere other than mom and dad's basement but are unable, or disinclined, to purchase a home? Well, they rent one—but the construction slowdown has been pushing rents higher at even a faster clip than home prices. Is there any relief in sight?

Possibly, if the industry and government and financiers can get their act together. The era of overregulation that followed the housing crisis has contributed to the pent-up demand, and we now see a movement toward deregulation that could begin to stimulate construction. But even that, and increased flexibility from HUD, will not resolve all the issues surrounding construction, leaving us with the stark fact that new construction still isn't close to fully meeting demand.

For those of us living in urban areas, it might seem there's a crane at every corner, but fewer apartments have been built in our country in the past decade than during any decade in a half century. In fact, there were fewer homes built in any year in the last decade than every single year between 1968 and 2007, with the exception of 1982. Meanwhile, new households have been forming at the pace of about one million a year for the past three years and are expected to keep up that pace.[40] Where will they live?

The current situation is dire, but where there are problems there are always opportunities. The need is immediate and urgent, and we

---

40   "The State of the Nation's Housing 2018," Joint Center for Housing Studies, Harvard University, http://www.jchs.harvard.edu/sites/default/files/Harvard_JCHS_State_of_the_Nations_Housing_2018.pdf.

must make it our business to truly help. America's urban centers are where the action is. In these cities, and the metropolitan regions that connect them, are the economic, cultural, and social support systems required for good community housing. The demand for affordability in these places is insatiable. At Grubb Properties, our team is working creatively and thoughtfully to address the housing shortfall and the affordability crisis that comes with it. Our goal is to identify and execute on strategies to drive down the cost of housing and provide people with safe and stable homes, a critical component of a healthy community.

The future looks extremely bright for businesses focused on value-based housing, given the enormous demand for it in coming years.

The future looks extremely bright for businesses focused on value-based housing, given the enormous demand for it in coming years. For investors, this segment of the market represents solid and extended returns with much lower risk. These conditions can support a long-term flow of capital, the kind that will be needed to make a meaningful difference. Grubb Properties is committed to this, and it has become a driving mission in my life. Many others across our great country are already working in this space, but we need many more to succeed.

It starts with awareness, but it can't stop there. We need a groundswell of advocacy to build community support for political and social change. We also need engagement. There are so many roles that people can play, such as directly volunteering with community housing organizations and pushing our political and business leaders to change entrenched laws, regulations, and policies. Many in the industry believe that regulations alone account for 30 percent of housing costs and as much as 40 percent of the construction schedule.

For individual investors and institutions, committing capital in this segment of the alternative market space is both compassionate and smart. It's an investment supported by demographic demand and protected by collateral investment in our urban centers today.

I think back on the challenges that my father faced when he committed to being a part of the solution in 1963, the year our company was founded. America today is so much more supportive than the Jim Crow South that he knew. The challenges today are great, but the possibilities are even greater. A stable home is the foundation for a family's health and security and the well-being of our communities. I urge everyone to participate in this endeavor. The success of our country and the stability of our future generations depend on it.

IDEAS TO SOLVE THE CRISIS

| *If you treat unequal people equally in the end you get unequal people.*

Arthur Griffin

I HOPE YOU ENJOYED the stories in my book and appreciated the importance of this issue. My goal is that everyone comes away with ideas to improve the situation.

If we were to set out today with a clean slate to create a comprehensive community housing framework, would the result be HUD and the myriad state and local agencies and departments that we have today? The answer, of course, is no. These inefficient bureaucracies were built over decades and are entangled with our history of poor public housing policy, segregation, and uncoordinated public and private investment or lack thereof. From the federal level to the local level, we need a clear and cohesive framework.

Below I outline ideas for folks to consider and explore in hopes that they keep the dialogue going. Some of them are controversial and others are less so, but most have substantial financial impact and are opportunities to immediately improve our housing affordability crisis.

Ideas to Moderate Construction Cost

- Sensible immigration policies

- Union participation in lowering high skill/high cost labor components through innovation

- National construction trade apprenticeship programs

- Transparent building inspections that are posted publicly

- State-level versus municipality-level plan reviews to promote consistency, which would significantly enhance the opportunity for more modular construction

Ideas to Create More Efficient and Affordable Housing

- Liberalize 4 percent tax credit program to have 50 percent of the community market-rate housing

- Expand transit investment in tandem with land-use policy

- Put the pedestrian, the bicycle, and the scooter ahead of the car in urban areas

- Eliminate parking minimums

- Eliminate setbacks and side yards and allow development to occur on small and odd lots

Ideas to Create Equity

- Expand the earned income tax credit

- Create a unified credit as a safety net for all Americans

- Provide coverage for all Americans to get doctor and dental checkups yearly, what I consider health education

- Expand education to cover every child starting at birth; the first three years are the most critical

Ideas to Free Up Resources and Streamline Bureaucracies

- Stop building new roads and other infrastructure that encourage sprawl and auto dependency

- Eliminate the federal Department of Housing and Urban Development

- Eliminate the child tax credit

- Eliminate the mortgage interest deduction

- Create stable neighborhoods to eliminate the cradle-to-prison pipeline

- Eliminate the 9 percent tax credit housing program

- Legalize euthanasia and eliminate capital punishment

- Eliminate all private prisons and reward rehabilitation, not reincarceration

Ideas to Provide Intelligent Financing Solutions and New Housing Finance Regulatory Framework

- Utility-based financing to improve efficiency of all homes and buildings

- Liberalize the power grid so that everyone is encouraged to generate power

- Set up emergency home equity lines of credit for when life happens

- Modify the home loan guarantee program to create equity and provide greater access to those who need it most. In other words, provide greater access to financing based on the lower cost of the home, not based on higher earnings by the borrower

- Replace down payments with emergency savings accounts